# WE WERE HERE

# WE WERE HERE
## Sexuality, Photography, and Cultural Difference
### SELECTED WRITINGS BY SUNIL GUPTA

*An Aperture Ideas Book*

*aperture*

# Contents

MIGRATIONS AND ARCHIVES
2013–2019

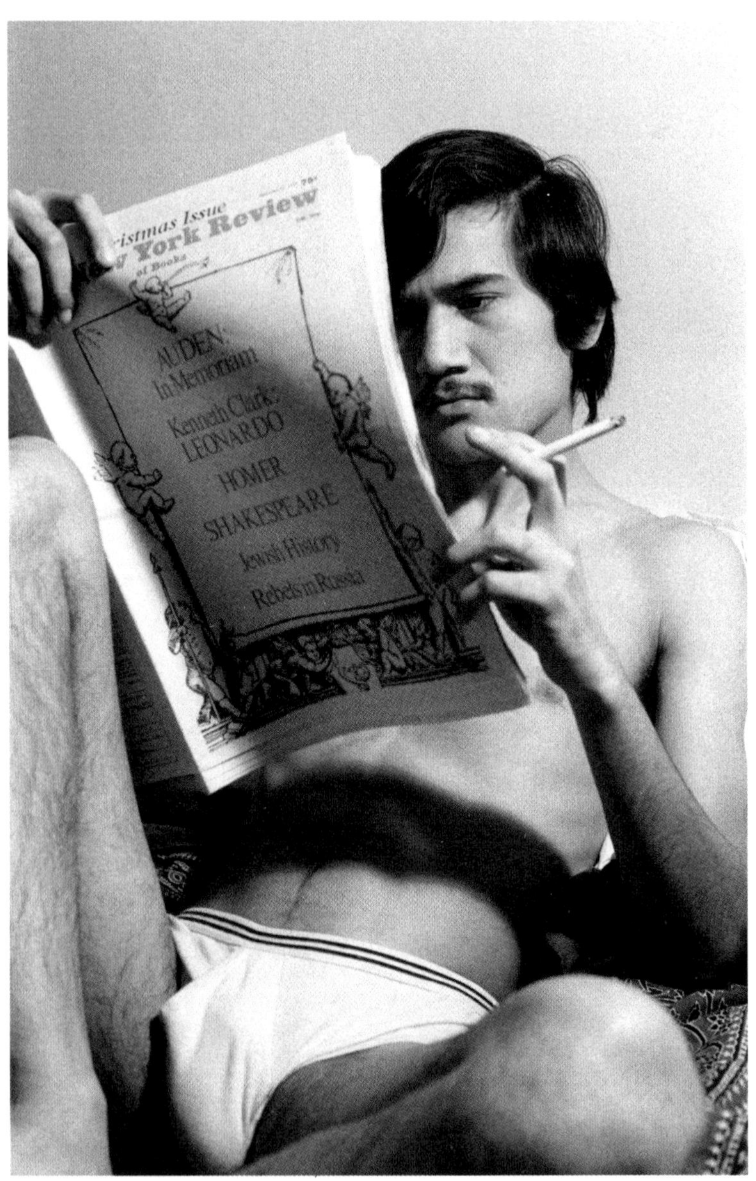


Sunil Gupta, Me with *The New York Review of Books*, 1972

# *Foreword*
# Theo Gordon

In 2004, the Jamaican sociologist and cultural theorist Stuart Hall credited Sunil Gupta with being a photographer whose images had changed what it was possible to see and desire in a queer, postcolonial world. Yet until now, the role of Gupta's writing in this process has been less widely known. This book is a contribution to the archival future of Gupta's practice, demonstrating that alongside his pathbreaking photographic and curatorial work over the last fifty years, he has also been a prolific, insightful, and witty writer. *We Were Here* shows how Gupta's writing has played a crucial role in creating new conjunctures of photography, sexuality, and cultural difference for decades, enabling a huge range of contemporary practices across multiple continents. Gupta has often written in moments of political pressure, publishing in diverse places, including ephemeral media such as magazines and community newsletters. *We Were Here* presents a selection of essays in more permanent form, divided into four sections that chart how Gupta's concerns have developed according to shifts in personal and geopolitical situations.

*We Were Here* begins with Gupta's first publication on homosexuality in India, in the *Guardian* in 1982. Having emigrated from India to Canada in 1969, Gupta arrived in London in 1977 to study at the West Surrey College of Art and Design (now University for the Creative Arts Farnham). In 1980, he won a travel award from Thames Television, enabling him to return to visit India for the first time. Having participated in the formation of public gay identities in the heady days of liberation in Montreal and New York in the early 1970s, he was struck by the furtive silence that surrounded gay sex in New Delhi, where "unnatural" sexual acts remained outlawed by Section 377, a legacy of British colonial rule.

Back in London, Gupta became involved in gay and Black organizing—"Black" understood in the 1980s British sense of political commitment and affiliation uniting people of South Asian, Afro-Caribbean, and African descent in the face of pervasive British racism. While completing an MA at the Royal College of Art in 1983, he participated in staging the first show of Black students' work there, to which the group invited members of the left-leaning Greater London Council's Race Equality Unit. This encounter with "town hall" politics was crucial to the subsequent trajectory of Gupta's work. He became a key figure in several movements that characterized Britain in the 1980s: insurgent Black cultural activism, critical photography practices, and gay and lesbian politics amid the burgeoning AIDS crisis. The essays in the book's first section, "Struggles for Representation in London," testify to his central role in breaking down barriers in Black photography and establishing institutions such as Autograph ABP to support it, all in the face of the social onslaught of Thatcherism and widespread indifference to Black cultural production in the UK.

The reconstitution of the European Economic Community as the European Union in February 1992 and the establishment of the Institute of International Visual Arts (Iniva) in London in 1994 reconfigured the landscape of Black cultural politics in Britain. Funded following years of wrangling with the Arts Council, Iniva represented the reluctant institutionalization of multicultural arts policy, in the wider context of the fall of communism and rise of globalization, and the end of apartheid in South Africa. In 1992, Gupta was awarded one of Iniva's new curatorial franchises, a prelude to the institute's formal establishment. He set up his own limited company, the Organisation for Visual Arts (OVA), to curate exhibitions of contemporary work by artists from varied "non-European" contexts, aiming to expand the display of visual art beyond the outdated frame of the NATO alliance. The essays in the second section, "New Internationalism and the New Europe," span the lifetime of OVA's existence and represent a fraction of Gupta's extraordinary curatorial output during this period, including exhibitions of the work of Hiram To, Stan Douglas, Fernando Arias, and Joy Gregory, as well as several international group shows. (His final OVA project was an exhibition of Roshini Kempadoo's work, which opened at Leicester City Art Gallery in 2004.) Gupta's early optimism about the possibilities of curating as cultural activism appears to wane, however; in later essays he laments the hegemonic British art world's inability to engage with the AIDS crisis and slams its continued ignorance of Black artists. His review of the retrospective book *Shades of Black* stands as an important reminder of the art world's recalcitrance to anyone who uncritically celebrates the ludicrously belated reception of Black arts in Britain in the late 2010s.

In 2005, Gupta returned to live in New Delhi for the first time since his teenage departure in 1969. This migration marked a decisive shift in his concerns and practice, precipitated by the unexpectedly popular reception of his exhibition *Pictures from Here*, curated by Radhika Singh, in Delhi in 2004. The essays collected in the book's third section, "Queer Delhi," show Gupta's immersion in the new queer politics in India, vitalized by a younger generation of activists, and in the consolidation of the contemporary practice and historical study of photography in South Asia. His playful journalism, while challenged by censorship in Delhi, nonetheless charts a dramatic shift in attitudes toward sexuality in India, marked for Gupta by the widespread youthful adoption of queer identifications. The first striking down of Section 377 in 2009, legalizing homosexuality in India, was a euphoric moment, thwarted by its later reversal by the Supreme Court in 2013. Gupta's activism and photography during this period—deeply informed by these political circumstances and by meeting his partner, the photographer Charan Singh—were also richly intertwined with his curatorial work. In 2007, with Radhika Singh and Gauri Gill, he established the magazine *Camerawork Delhi*, and proceeded to cocurate *Click! Contemporary Photography in India* with Singh in Delhi in 2008. *Where Three Dreams Cross: 150 Years of Photography from India, Pakistan and Bangladesh*, cocurated with Singh, Hammad Nasar, Shahidul Alam, and Kirsty Ogg, followed in London in 2010. It is ironic, given his huge contributions to establishing the field of contemporary photography in India, that it was the controversy surrounding the display of his own work in Delhi that precipitated his next migration. The Delhi police raided the exhibition of his sensuous series *Sun City* (2010), set in a Parisian bathhouse, charging the work as "obscene" and against "Hindu culture," leading Gupta to return to London in 2013.

The essays in the final section, "Migrations and Archives," show Gupta's reflections on the connections, identities, and horizons of political possibility established over fifty years of his critical practice. Of particular significance is "Queer Migrations," an abridged version of Gupta's doctoral dissertation, published here for the first time. In it he theorizes how his series *Homelands* (2001–3), *Mr Malhotra's Party* (2007), *Sun City* (2010), and *The New Pre-Raphaelites* (2010) register "two kinds of migration . . . the physical movement between countries and cultures, and the singular psychological movement toward a gay identity." In Gupta's liberatory practice, solidarity and connection cause narrow national, racial, and sexual divisions to melt away. Just as he submitted his dissertation in 2018, Section 377 was struck down by the Supreme Court of India for a second and final time.

*We Were Here* testifies to the strength and endurance of Gupta's efforts in photography and cultural activism, showing that while his queer, postcolonial work has been differently inflected by shifting circumstances over time, his concerns with pleasure, beauty, and reimagining the world have remained constant.

One note for readers: The essays that follow have been edited and updated for this volume; however, special care has been taken to preserve the printing of the words *black* and *Black* as they appeared in original publication, to convey the political specificity of the latter term in Britain in the 1980s. It has been a pleasure to work on this book with Sunil, and my heartfelt thanks go to him and Charan Singh for making the process so enjoyable.

*London, May 2022*

Theo Gordon is an art historian and lecturer in contemporary art and photography based in London.

# *Struggles for Representation in London 1982–1992*

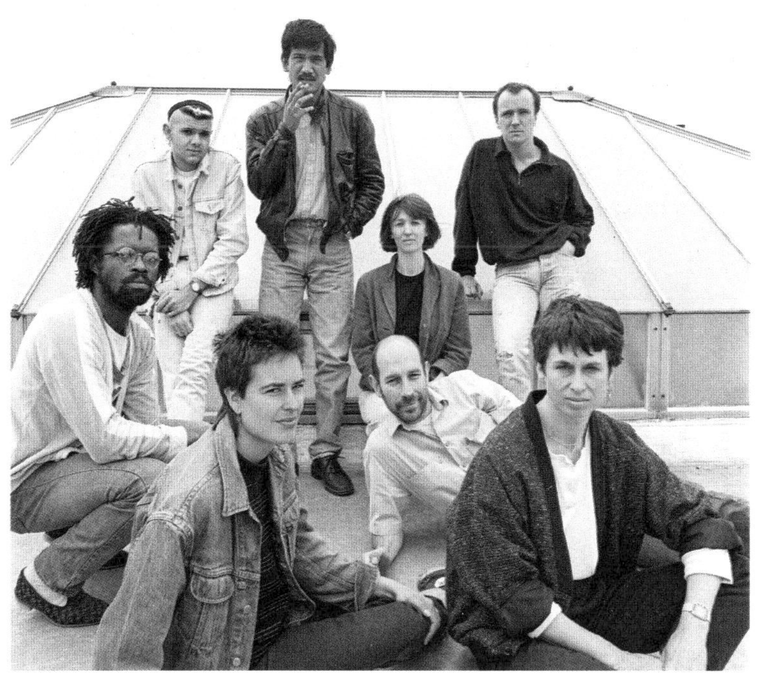

Sunil Gupta, A group of the lesbian and gay artist-photographers who took part in the exhibition *Same Difference* at Camerawork, London, 1986

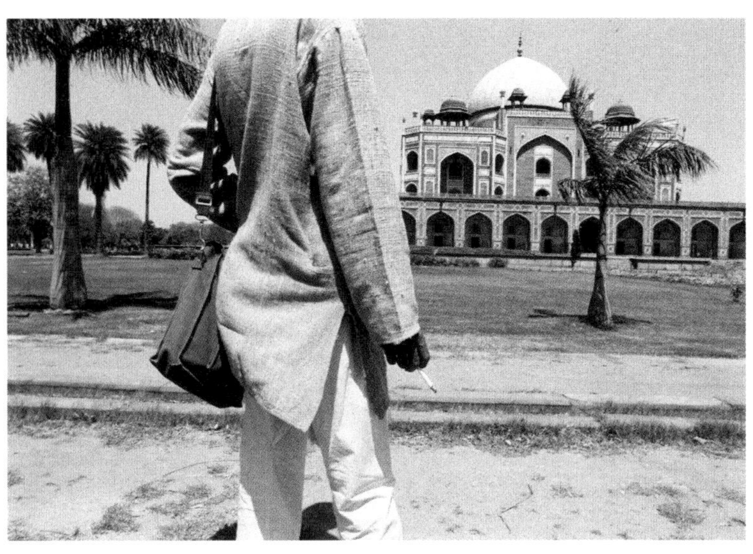

Sunil Gupta, *Humayun's Tomb, Towards an Indian Gay Image*, Delhi, 1982

# *They Dare Not Speak Its Name in Delhi: On the Secret Suffering of India's Homosexual Community*

One of the best kept secrets in India is the practice of homosexuality, although there is no lack of practitioners from all social classes. While there are definitely no openly homosexual people in public life, the activity is concentrated in the big cities, and among the educated classes a gay subculture is beginning to be recognized. Operating through a network of personal contacts, its public face is limited—in Delhi, for example—to a park in the city center.

Always, there is a fear of discovery. The sanctions appear to come from all communities, who blame each other for introducing the practice. Hindus claim the Muslims brought it, though references to it can be found in Hindu mythology. Muslims believe that they found it within a decadent Hindu culture, while everyone agrees that the West is exporting it.

It is defined almost exclusively as sodomy. There being no equivalents to *gay*, *lesbian*, or *homosexual* in the vernacular languages, the reference in Hindi remains specific to sodomy, frequently appearing as an abuse. Women homosexuals appear not to exist.

Indian society, being a mass of contradictions and double standards, requires the individual to dedicate their life to presenting a conventional puritanical public image. Sexual segregation ensures that men and women do not meet outside the arranged marriage. Meanwhile, public displays of physical contact within the same sex groupings are tolerated. Deviation is frowned upon and discouraged by the economies of living within a family.

This leads to confusion, as most supposedly homosexual men are married, and many supposedly heterosexual married men indulge in casual homosexual sex. An exclusively gay identity does not seem possible, particularly since there is a great unwillingness to discuss sexuality. Besides, there is no information about homosexuality, except that which filters through the popular Western press. The Indian media is devoid of any references, except indirectly as a rare editorial survey of, for example, what college students think about it, in the English-language press. The vernacular press is not known to have published anything at all, while the film industry has never treated the subject.

More recently, the revolutionary fervor that has overtaken the thinking of many of the educated youth has led to a spread of feminist ideology which, in turn, is spawning an awareness of lesbianism. Paradoxically, the supposedly nonexistent homosexual women now have a better chance of identifying themselves as lesbians.

Some men also now define themselves as being gay (although most view marriage as an inevitable duty), and a few have chosen not to marry. Both men and women see the cloak of uncertainty as a guarantee of their freedom in the present political climate. This uncertainty extends to the law. Everyone assumes that homosexual acts are illegal, but no one is really sure. Despite a lack of documented cases, the police seem to operate a system of harassment and extortion, with payment sometimes being in the form of sexual services.

There are prominent homosexual people in Delhi, members of parliament, journalists, academics, and others, who could campaign for gay rights; but being immune within the Indian system of rank and patronage, satisfying their needs through privilege, they think it unnecessary to initiate change.

Meanwhile, caste and class prevent the formation of an autonomous group identity. Even in the park, where to be seen is to be discovered, there are divisions along the usual Indian lines. Most people who have choice, mostly men of the middle and upper classes, prefer to maintain a conventional façade, exploiting children, prostitutes, employees, or anyone over whom they have power to satisfy their sexual needs.

If their wives discover the truth, they do not have a channel to express it. Neither can they afford to lose the status of marriage, even though some husbands may terminate sexual relations. Indeed, some men have entered marriages without any intention of ever sleeping with their wives.

Since for nearly all Indians, the prospect of losing jobs and the support of their families is untenable, the gay subculture waits for signs of a movement. But those who could lead it have the least incentive to do so. The radical youth argue that in India there are larger issues, but they cannot answer the question of whether there can be revolution without sexual liberation.

Revolution in nearby Iran has meant the death penalty for homosexuality. As religious fundamentalism grows within India, those who have kept their sexuality secret may have reason to be thankful. Others, who cannot live within the network of lies and corruption, either have to leave the country or give up their sexuality altogether.

Originally published in the *Guardian*, Third World Review, November 26, 1982.

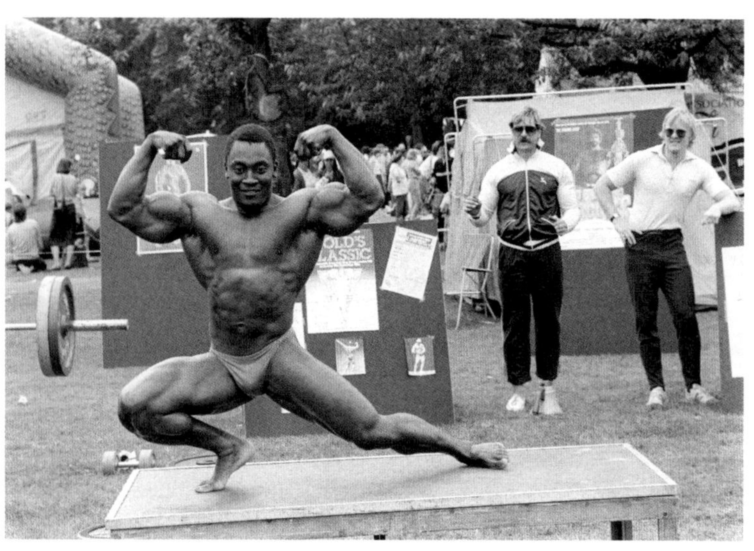

Sunil Gupta, Battersea Park, London, 1984

# Desire and Black Men

The discourses around desire and Blacks very rarely overlap, and even less so in terms of photographic representation. There are several reasons for this: The theoretical discussions around desire/sexuality have limited themselves to a white discussion around sexual difference rather than discussion of the *difference* of sexual orientation; and from a Black perspective, sexual orientation is viewed as a white issue and Black gays are seen to have turned their backs on Black struggle. Furthermore, in the current climate against "pornography" and the AIDS scare, to want to reconstruct a positive image of Black gay male desire is a delicate matter.

Several recent events in London, sponsored by the Greater London Council, have begun to tie these disparate elements together. A conference held at the Brixton Recreation Centre in mid-February 1986 titled "Black Communities: Living & Struggling Together" addressed itself to the differences within the Black community, principally of sexual orientation. Black lesbians and gay men came together with Black heterosexuals to discuss the issues that divide us. Although the heterosexual turnout was very small, one vociferous man reminded us all day how we had "caught a white disease."

In March, two photographic shows opened: one titled *Reflections of the Black Experience* at Brixton Art Gallery, and one titled *Darshan* at Camerawork. I participated in both of these shows.

The Brixton show was commissioned work and, while I got lesbian and gay issues on the agenda, there was only one photograph that referred to a gay presence, out of a hundred. Faced with a choice of making ten photographs around the Black gay male experience or ten around key issues facing people of South Asian descent in the UK, I chose the latter. I admit, in this instance, to have given in to the pressure to marginalize sexual politics in favor of communal politics within the Black framework.

The Camerawork show was organized out of existing work, and since it was by and about South Asians, I felt freer about presenting a set of photographs representing the sexuality of Indian men. In this show, I was literally the one in ten, but I felt comfortable, as the cultural identity of the show had already been defined.

Both these shows are being read as historic and as first steps to establishing a Black presence within the British photographic community. Having been through these experiences, I would like to concentrate my work on the reconstruction of a Black gay male image of desire, keeping in mind that the audience is not only going to be the photographic community but also the Black community at large. One of the lessons learned by Black gays after more than a decade of working for gay liberation is that not only does the movement marginalize Blacks, in a mirror image of society, but there is a pressing need to educate the Black community that we exist, and a wish to reintegrate ourselves with the communities that we came from. In my own work, it has meant returning to the city that I grew up in, Delhi, in order to make photographs that reflect the gay experience over there. Here in Britain, I would like to work on a series of photographs that allow Black gay men to construct an image of themselves as both producers and consumers of sexual desire.

Historically, Black men have appeared in popular picture magazines as objects of desire. For the purposes of this article, I'll begin with the "physique" and "fitness" magazines of the '50s and '60s.[1] These follow a European tradition of photographing the male nude in classical settings. They appeared in North

America and Britain, although it was in the US that repressive laws surrounding representation were successfully fought and won. The European tradition of setting out to the Mediterranean countries to find examples of idealized youth and beauty[2] also fitted the photographers who were able to distance themselves from their Northern homes. Black models begin to appear in the '50s, perhaps to coincide with the first wave of migrants from the West Indies. Curiously, the only Asians to make an occasional appearance are East Asians. I assume that South Asians either were not interested in bodybuilding or, more likely, that there was no demand for them. Although clearly aimed at a male gay audience, these magazines assiduously avoid revealing any part of male genitalia. This was due to the political climate of their times, an atmosphere of sexual repression which was not challenged until the late '60s and prevails to this day in Britain.

The '40s and '50s—best known for postwar reconstruction in Europe, the Cold War and McCarthyism in the US, and independence and hope in colonized countries—are not normally thought of as a time of debate around sexual representation. It was a time when men were men, and women were women, and Blacks were meant to be kept in their place. Still, the climate allowed for the production and distribution of these magazines emphasizing the body beautiful, gay male sexuality, and desire. In the '50s, in the US, the magazines won a significant legal battle to allow them distribution through the US Postal Service.[3]

It must be pointed out that the magazines were produced by and for a white audience. The images of Blacks blend in with a popular reading of white classical treatments. So, we have "Howard Hunter" leaning against a Greco-Roman pillar, as we have "George Paine" doing something similar. "Leroy Colbert—a smiling young Titan: by Lon" gets the full treatment in an extended piece titled "A Modern Hercules," prefaced by a reproduction of the *Farnese Hercules*. Leroy is described as a happy person with no complexes and, in case we read a gay subtext into the piece, he is reported to just have fathered Hercules III. Other photo-captions describe him as "Massive Power in Controlled Repose," or "The Strength of the Hills is His Also." *Modern Man* in 1959 brings us "From Jamaica, Neville Chisholm," who leans against a pillar and gazes up with a slight expression of bewilderment. Perhaps he was surprised at his facing page, which offers us two stereotyped pictures of "Natives": one from the Pacific and one from the Bahamas. "Noel Chaffey," it tells us, "sends these startling pictures of untrained men." No doubt untrained in the sense of weight training, but with a clear reference to untrained as in "uncivilized."

Sometimes the images have a camp sensibility, like "Cecil Addison," who looks like a Black incarnation of Errol Flynn, complete with sword. By the '60s in the US, both color and penises began to appear, although, in accordance with the rules, erections were still not allowed. Where more than one man appears in the photograph, the rule limiting contact to a straight wrestling variety has been relaxed to introduce definite gay iconography, such as overtones of S&M, uniforms, and touching. Now the photographs are clearly made for a gay male audience. In one, "David Boyle & Jim Davis" gaze into each other's eyes, with their thighs touching in a romantic outdoor setting shot in a studio. An ideal cover shot for a gay Mills & Boon romance, Jim Davis is Black. Romance has overtaken beefcake. An even more amazing picture, since the Black man appears to be literally on an equal footing with the white man; if anything, the Black man appears in a dominant position, as he leans toward the white man while offering his thigh for support. In 1969, Black drag queens were in the forefront of the riots around the Stonewall Inn in New York that marked the birth of the Gay Liberation Movement.

In the '60s and '70s, "deviants" appeared as "appropriate subject matter for art photographers" (Susan Sontag).[4] Diane Arbus's show at the Museum of Modern Art in New York, of 120 photographs, attracted a sizeable audience; and since her death in 1971, her book has been the best-selling monograph in the history of photographic publishing.[5] Roll film, square format, and deviant subject matter combined to produce two of the best

                    *DESIRE AND BLACK MEN*

known gay photographers, Robert Mapplethorpe and Arthur Tress. By the late '70s and early '80s, Mapplethorpe's work had gained widespread notoriety by representing marginal and extreme forms of sexuality, particularly homosexuality and Black men. This happened against a background of ever-increasing gains by the gay community in the US, the legalization of male homosexuality in the UK for people over twenty-one in 1967, and a growing number of pictorial publications aimed at the gay male market. The physique poses have given way to a variety of macho styles: cowboys, construction workers, and clones. Every conceivable kind of gay male sex has been photographed; the debate around representation within the gay movement has revolved around the need to stimulate desire and the desirability of limiting sexual role models to just a few stereotypes.

As the political climate changed with Reaganism in the US and Thatcherism in Britain, the agents of sexual repression restarted their work. Clean physique poses reclaim our attention, as in the work of Bruce Weber. Ads for permanent hair removal litter the back pages of the US's gay magazines. And AIDS has emerged, in the eyes of some, as retribution. We have seen the gains of the '70s swept away, we are under attack from the anti-"pornography" lobby, we have been returned to the laboratory by the medical researchers.

In this climate exist the photographs of Robert Mapplethorpe, author of an exhibition and catalogue titled *Black Males*.[6] Following Western art traditions, Mapplethorpe is a sculptor by training; he has photographed Black men essentially as objects. While this may make formalist sense, for us as Black consumers, he continues in the tradition of white photographers who have appropriated the Black image in order to reinforce the mythologies surrounding Black men; that in terms of desire, they are limited to physique and big dicks. Initially, I was very interested in Mapplethorpe's work as an art student in the UK, as there seemed little or no work that seemed of specific interest to me. The nearest we got to exposure to his images was in a history lecture where his work was referred to but not shown; the student body was deemed too young or impressionable. I found this coyness very irritating, since we were constantly bombarded by the nudes of Edward Weston and Bill Brandt.

Eventually, I used some of his imagery in an audiovisual work about the history of London Gay Switchboard in an attempt to punctuate the narrative with a discourse about gay male art photography. This resulted in a ban on showing it after I showed it to members of the Switchboard collective. Several very vocal members found the images very offensive. I realized that if members of the gay community were offended, I could hardly expect my college (Farnham) to enter into a discussion around gay male desire, let alone Black gay male desire. Throughout my experience as a student and then a postgraduate student, I have found the issues that I specifically wanted to deal with marginalized. The all-white, heterosexual staff had, at best, formalism to offer.

It is on these grounds that Mapplethorpe has gained widespread acceptance. A recent article in *Aperture* follows that line as it traces the "human geometry" in Mapplethorpe's work. *Jimmy Freeman* (1981) shows a Black man sitting on his haunches with his forearms crossing his ankles; he wears a white skullcap, and his dick hangs down and intersects with his ankles or, as *Aperture* puts it, "The phallus forms a plinth for the nude, intersecting a triangular white space and penetrating ankles and forearms. Here the abstracted head is made contiguous with the abstracted phallus (a Black line)."[7] Is Jimmy a dickhead, masquerading as a Black line?

*Man in Polyester Suit* (1981) and *Jack, Fire Island* (1982) carry on in a similar vein. Headless Jack offers us his dick, since handily it lies at the apex of the geometry of his body. "Fire Island" suggests a gay venue; "The Pines" would have clinched it. Assuming then that Jack is gay and that the image, with its outdoor location and Jack's boots, refers to a gay pictorial tradition, the audience for this work must be gay males and the art world cognoscenti. This relentless offering of the nude Black male as a sacrificial

     *DESIRE AND BLACK MEN*

figure can become tedious. Sometimes though, he does offer us a photograph with more meaning. *Man in Polyester Suit*, for me, sits on the edge of being yet another big Black dick, and a more complex reference to Black men in culture. We have seen images of Black men in suits, but the emphasis on polyester defines their position in society. I have to admit that in this instance, the contrast of textures between the artificiality of the material and the softness of the skin, the parallel veins in the penis and the hand, and the caress of the white shirt over the penis, works for me. *Abbraccio* (1982) depicts a Black man and a white man locked in an embrace with their pants on. "David Boyle" and "Jim Davis" no longer have to reveal their genitals and are allowed to carry their touching into an embrace suggesting an emotional life. Progress.

During three trips to India over the last few years, I have been trying to develop a pictorial scheme that could begin to relate the experience of gay men there. There was a time, growing up in Delhi, when I thought that only Indian men had sex with each other. Arriving in the West in 1969 in the wake of Stonewall, I found the Gay Liberation Movement an easy way of working out my identity. It was a time when you thought that everyone was working together toward the common goal of liberation. Cultural and generational gaps with one's family were relatively easily sorted out as one built bridges within the gay community. In the long run, the family and cultural differences have proved to be very resilient, and the gay movement and the expansion of the gay scene have shown themselves to be primarily aimed at a white middle-class male audience. Returning to photograph in India gave me a great sense of purpose. Here, at least, I was not marginalized by skin color, and the issues seemed very clear on a range of problems. I set about contacting the gay community there and discovered, first of all, that as a very complex society, India would only allow me access to urban middle-class men vis-à-vis a discussion around sexuality. And then, to take photographs in a society where your social identity is paramount was very threatening. The only public face of the gay network there is the variety of public meeting places, since there is no "scene" as in the Western model. The solution I have come up with is to work with men who are prepared to volunteer for the project. We pick a particular known location and reconstruct a scene. This gives me the chance to pick suitable light conditions and to try out a variety of angles. I hope, eventually, to cover the range of people and places that comprise a facet of the gay experience in India. The models are anonymous to both protect their identities and also to emphasize the invisibility of gay men in India.

*Humayun's Tomb* (1982, see page 16) was first published in the *Guardian*, and I wrote an explanatory text to go with it. It was also, most recently, the basis of my contribution to the Camerawork show about South Asians.[8]

Happily, the question of doing "physique" type nudes does not arise in India, since the body is not idealized in quite the same way. Clothing and other cultural signifiers work to stimulate desire. Although there is a demand for imagery from the West and a history of erotic sculpture, the current climate is very repressive in terms of sexual desire. In any event, a direct representation of sexuality in India can be easily sensationalized by the media here in the UK, as Mary Ellen Mark's work on the "cages" in Bombay was in the *Sunday Times*.[9]

In the UK, my work in response to Mapplethorpe and others has been to investigate the other possibilities of meaning that being gay and/or Black might suggest. The photograph of the bodybuilder in Battersea works because of the two white men who hover in the background, who act as his trainers or possibly "civilizers," and who define the limit of his possibilities. Recently, a white commercial agent suggested making a poster out of the image by leaving out the two white men to make it commercially viable. Here, always, there is the dichotomy of race.

A recent issue of the *New York Native* contains an invaluable document of the voices of Black brothers and sisters.[10] Although they live in another country and have had quite different histories to ours, what they have to say holds in general to our experiences as well. We left our homes and cultures in the belief that within the gay movement, we would find a just cause in which we could participate as equals. But in the end, we discovered that white gay men suffer from the racism that permeates society at large. We now must return to the cultures that we came from with the news that we are gay. We must begin a dialogue with our own communities. *We have to conquer our fear of organizing in our own communities.* Black lesbians are saying to the women's movement that, *if you want us, you must take our men too.* The biggest challenge is to gain acceptance of the fact that being gay is not a white disease. As the writing on a piece of artwork puts it, "they say there were no gays in Africa before the white man, well then where did I inherit this Black male gay spirit?"

One of the unfortunate legacies of colonialism has been the criminalization of male homosexuality. These codes remain in India and in most other countries, and although "homosexual acts between consenting adults were decriminalized in Zaire in 1984, [it] hasn't stopped the arrests and blackmail of men assumed to be gay. Cops have virtually unlimited powers to keep people imprisoned indefinitely without charge or trial."[11]

Now, there is a new scourge to haunt us. AIDS. In the debate over whether it originated in Zaire or the bathhouses of New York and San Francisco, Black gay men find themselves the unfocused center of attention. Initially identified as a gay disease, AIDS educators ignored the Black communities, whereas in fact, the rates of AIDS for Blacks in the US have been disproportionately high. There are twice as many AIDS cases among Blacks there than the proportion Blacks make up of the total population.[12] With the attack on gay sexuality under the guise of AIDS education in full swing, it's going to be important to fight to retain our right to define our own identity, and to fight the legal and censorship battles now going on in the UK.

Victor Burgin has argued for a "politics of representation" rather than a "representation of politics."[13] He has also argued for showing the meaning of sexual difference and desire as a process of production: as something mutable, something historical, and therefore something we can do something about. I'm arguing, then, that given the emerging framework of a Black gay presence within a racist and homophobic society, it's time we reconstructed images of desire by ourselves and for ourselves.

*Thanks to Simon Watney.*

Originally published in *Ten.8*, "Black Experiences," January 1986.

Notes

1   *Modern Man*, March 1959; *Men and Art*, May 1958; *Star Models*, 1954; *Man's World*, May 1956; *Body Beautiful*, 1956–60; *Physique: A Pictorial History of the Athletic Model Guild*, ed. Winston Leyland (San Francisco: Gay Sunshine Press, 1982).

2   Paul Lewis, "Men on Pedestals," *Ten.8* 17 (January 1985): pp. 22–29.

3   *Before Stonewall: The Making of a Gay and Lesbian Community*, directed by Greta Schiller and Robert Rosenberg (New York: First Run Features, 1984), 87 min.

4   Susan Sontag, *On Photography* (New York: Farrar, Straus and Giroux, 1977).

5   Diane Arbus, *An Aperture Monograph* (New York: Aperture, 1972).

6   *Robert Mapplethorpe*, ed. Germano Celant (Venice: Comune di Venezia, 1983); *Robert Mapplethorpe 1970–1983*, ed. Sandy Nairne (London: Institute of Contemporary Arts, 1983).

7   Mike Weaver, "Mapplethorpe's Human Geometry: A Whole Other Realm," *Aperture*, The Human Street, Winter 1985, p. 44.

8   Sunil Gupta, "They Dare Not Speak Its Name in Delhi: Sunil Gupta on the Secret Suffering of India's Homosexual Community," *Guardian*, November 26, 1982. Reprinted in this volume, see page 16.

9   Mary Ellen Mark, "The Life of a Bombay Cage Girl," *Sunday Times Magazine*, May 24, 1981.

10  *New York Native*, A Heritage of Black Pride (supplement), March 3, 1986.

11  Editor's note: Gupta sourced this quotation from the gay press in London in 1986. The Democratic Republic of the Congo (DRC) was named the Republic of Zaire from 1971 to 1997. This quote is partially erroneous: homosexuality has never been illegal in the DRC, even as the Penal Code's restrictions against "crimes against family life" are used to persecute gay people, who enjoy limited protections against various forms of civic discrimination.

12  Philip M. Boffey, "Blacks Alerted on Risks of AIDS," *New York Times*, October 23, 1985, p. 28.

13  Victor Burgin, "Man-Desire-Image," in *Desire* (London: Institute of Contemporary Arts, 1984).

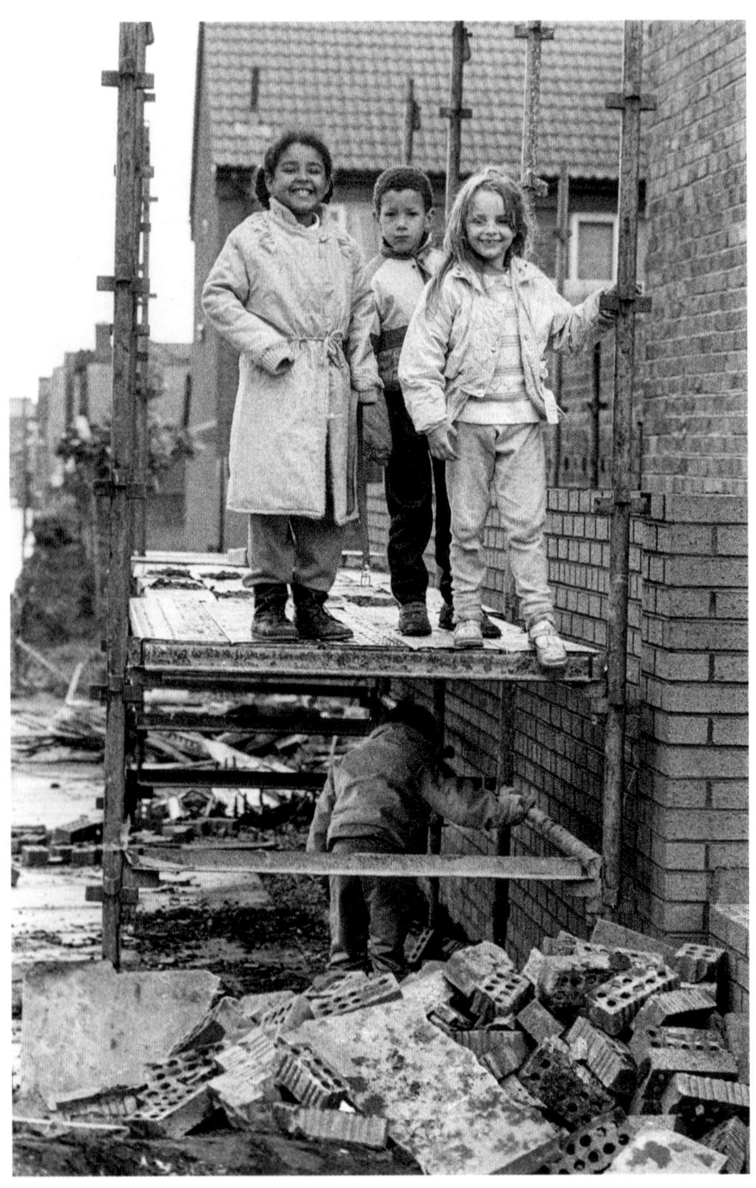

Sunil Gupta, Council Estate, Liverpool, for *New Society*, 1987

# Coincidental Commissions: Independent British Photography in the Late 1980s

Color as a suitable medium for the independent photographer in the UK has a very short history of about ten years. The Photographers' Gallery in London has gone from *Contemporary Colour Photography*, a group show presented in 1980 at "Salford '80" that went unnoticed, to *Mysterious Coincidences* in 1987, another group show with an international tour.

Independent photography has an even shorter history. The two have come to be almost synonymous through the work of Paul Graham and Martin Parr—Graham's *Troubled Land* (1984–86) has been widely exhibited and is available as a book. As a parallel development, women photographers have been making steady inroads as well. The work of Jo Spence has gained a wider audience with the publication of her book *Putting Myself in the Picture* (1987). Commissions provide a lot of the impetus for the production of new work in this field, therefore it is not surprising that this is how Anna Fox's project *Work Stations* came into being. What's surprising is its subject matter—office work.

It is surprising on many counts. It is against the grain of current fashion, which veers toward the private psychological scenario—as in the series of large color photographs of herself in different guises by Cindy Sherman, acquired by the Tate Gallery in 1983. Women photographers are rarely seen to engage with "work," and if they do, they have often limited themselves to specifically "women's issues." The photographic treatment of "work" in the UK has often meant a return to the cloth-capped working-class image in the North and Midlands.

Black-and-white photography has held its ground over color because of commercial and aesthetic considerations. Not only is it cheaper to produce and disseminate, but it also has a direct link with the history of the medium, and has the ability to abstract and dramatize a situation. Color has had many problems, including expense and a tendency to glamourize, and in doing so, trivialize.

Anna Fox is emerging from a very recent trend of color photographers: to marry the tradition of documentary photography with the formal concerns of art photography, where work is principally aimed at the gallery audience and the book market. Although there was an explosion of interest in the new color work in the US in the mid-'70s, very little of it managed to cross the Atlantic. There was *Californian Colour* at the Photographers' Gallery in 1981, but mostly, this work was seen in book form. For example, two American color books edited by Sally Euclaire were very influential, of which *New Color/New Work* (1984) is the more recent.

Not only did color become acceptable, but the use of color negatives became legitimized as an alternative to transparency film and dye-transfer prints, previously the only materials known to be stable. The cost and complexity of this had been daunting, particularly since, in the UK, there never existed a network of dealers and buyers. The best opportunities photographers could hope for were grants and commissions, and these were never large enough to sustain a movement in color photography.

What is also lacking in Britain is institutional support or an influential figurehead to champion the cause of photography. The Museum of Modern Art in New York has played a leading role in establishing a place for the art form in America. John Szarkowski, the curator of photography, signaled the arrival of color photography in the art world in the mid-'70s by showing Stephen Shore's

*Uncommon Places*, a series of color landscapes of the American South shot on large-format negative film.

When the initial breakthrough did come in Britain, it came from artists working in a fine-art tradition. Conceptual artists began to use the camera—as in the case of Boyd Webb, who simply recorded his work—then realized that the photograph as an end in itself was more interesting.

There are sharp divisions of approach between professional photographers and professional artists, somewhat complicated by the English taste for "shamateurism," i.e., eccentricity with no professional background. "Straight" or professional British photographers tended to fare the worst in the struggle for recognition. They have been forced to hang on to a narrow notion of photography, which makes them unable to look beyond turn-of-the-century pictorialism and the old question, "Is photography art?" They have finely honed their craft in the world of editorial and advertising photography.

Editorial work has been the outlet for the great British tradition of photojournalism. The Sunday supplements have provided an important venue for color documentary photography. As a parallel development, freelance, cooperative agencies have proliferated. There is now a London Magnum office (the original and best-known photographic cooperative in the world), Network, Format (the only all-women agency), and a commercial all-color agency, Impact.

Set against these developments is the arrival of the term "independent" to describe an unrecognized professionalism in photography that appears to be a relative of "independent" filmmaking. Independent photographers seem to be doggedly pursuing a personal approach to photography in the face of all odds. There are no specific clients, no market or art buyers, just a notion of an interested audience.

A structure is being created for independent photographers, but how successful it will be in addressing their needs remains to be seen. The Independent Film and Video Association has expanded to become the Independent Film, Video & Photography Association, and is now working on a "code of practice" for photography. The Arts Council cannot decide whether to upgrade photography into an independent art form, and independent photography lacks the resources or backing to stand on its own feet.

Anna Fox describes herself as an "independent photographer," and *Work Stations* certainly follows the classic independent production pattern. With two institutional commissioners, private sponsorship, and help from the Arts Council, we have a new body of color work that appears both in exhibition and as a book. It is a classic commission story in that she was looking for support following her work on Basingstoke. As a Southerner familiar with the commuter belt around London, her work was developing around daily life in the new towns. She came to Camerawork just as the gallery was engaged in formulating a commission with the Museum of London on office life—partly because it had never been done, possibly because of its mundaneness, and partly to look at it from a woman's point of view. Other photographers were considered, but Anna was the most relevant.

Commissions are the lifeblood of independent photography. The devolution of the Arts Council's responsibility in this area to the Regional Arts Associations via the "Glory of the Garden" policy has resulted in a very uneven national availability of funding. Photographers in regions like the North East do extremely well, whereas in other areas, they are dependent on the enthusiasm of the officers and departments involved. This leaves local authorities and indirect funding via gallery commissions and the recently set-up Photographers' Gallery Trust Fund to take up the responsibility.

These days, the talk is of private sponsorship. The likelihood of direct corporate sponsorship of independent photography is slim. Galleries and other intervening bodies have a new role to play in finding sponsorship at an adequate level to keep the work flowing. Even more so because of the extremely interventionist line the government has taken with local authorities, imposing limiting

   *COINCIDENTAL COMMISSIONS*

criteria on their ability to fund work in specific areas—e.g., the "promotion" of homosexuality. Independent photography galleries have a vital new role to play in both providing the resources to make the work possible and in maintaining a distance between funders and photographers, to allow the work to progress in an unfettered way.

Anna Fox has worked in close relation with her commissioners, Camerawork and the Museum of London. Several meetings have taken place along the way and ideas exchanged. The geographical proximity of all concerned, not to mention the subject matter, has meant that she has been able to follow up new leads rapidly. *Work Stations* addresses issues of contemporary concern at several levels. The use of a narrative format to tell a story, as it were, deliberately engages the audience with a form that they are familiar with. It relates to the British documentary tradition, except that pictorial conventions of documentary photography (i.e., objective realism and preference for 35 mm format) have been turned on their head.

*Work Stations* seeks to claim yet more ground by its use of textual captions as an integral part of the work. Again, these are not the captions one traditionally associates with documentary photography (those that merely give descriptive information about the image), but require the audience to work on the connections suggested by image and text. Text sources are not literal quotes from people in the pictures, which creates a sense of theater.

Image-text is an established convention. The text can be rhetorical, polemic, or serve as a guide to the narrative. By placing the text, which is in the form of statements where we would normally expect to find a caption/quote from the subject of the photograph, Anna Fox is both subverting our expectations and creating a powerful statement about her attitude to office work. In her use of image-text then, she is borrowing more from the tradition of conceptual art than photojournalism.

Anna Fox cites, among the variety of influences on her photography, the work of American photographer Joel Sternfeld for his use of large-format color to record everyday occurrences, and Duane Michals for image-text. Although having experimented with handwritten captions as used by Michals, she has opted for the more objective use of printed text. Through this less personal style, she reveals her shared concern with other independent photographers who have been critical of the "work of art" becoming too precious.

*Work Stations* has shifted the site of struggle away from the traditional lines of class, and focused timely attention on the conflicts within offices. Its aesthetics are not those of magazines like *Management Today*, which continue to sell us an uncritical image in their use of photography. Yet they are appealing to a wider audience than *Office at Night* by Victor Burgin, published in *Between* (1987).

*Work Stations* was photographed on a Plaubel Makina 67 camera with a wide-angle lens on Fujicolor negative film. The flash was a Metz 45 CT. The film received standard processing in a commercial laboratory, and Anna made the prints herself on Fujicolor paper. Her captions originate from a wide variety of sources: sociology books, trade journals, newspapers, business magazines, and tape-recorded conversations with the office staff. Access to offices became possible because this was an official commission, and she enjoyed nearly one hundred percent positive responses to her inquiries. Some wanted her to photograph straight away, others needed an appointment, and sometimes she had to work under the watchful eye of public relations personnel.

Having worked in an office herself, armed with her research and her skill as a photographer, Anna's portrayal of office life as total war—where men do battle and women are relegated to supporting roles—is completely convincing. The feeling of aggression is carried through by her choice of text and the use of direct and all-revealing flash. She exposes the myriad details that go toward making an office space more appealing, and facial expressions not caught by the naked eye.

It is remarkable that in this climate of shrinking funding, young photographers are able to confront complex issues, find adequate backing, and emerge with success.

Originally published in Anna Fox, *Work Stations: Office Life in London* (London: Camerawork, 1988).

SUNIL GUPTA

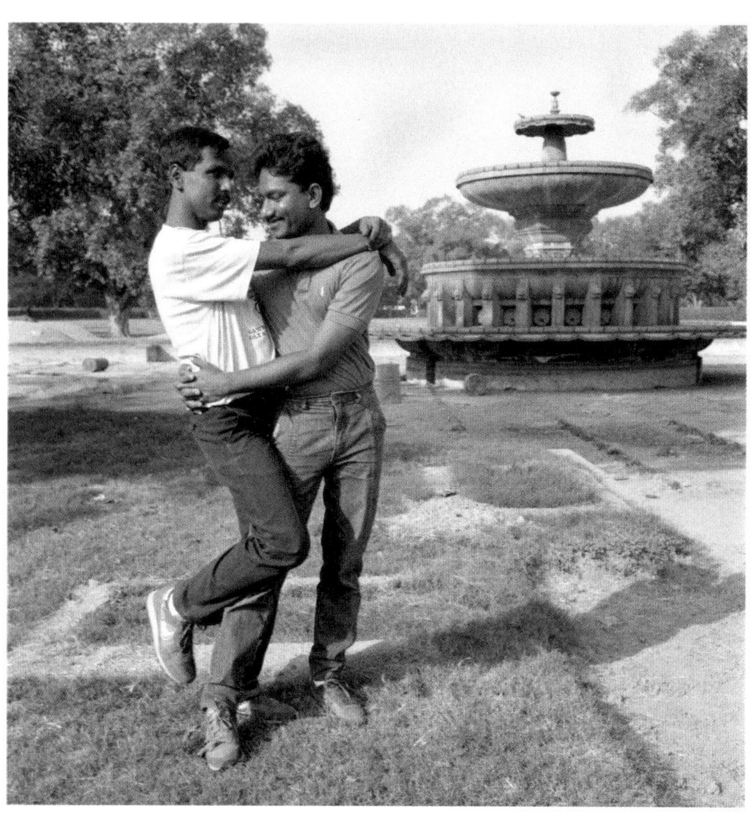

Sunil Gupta, Outtake from the series *Exiles*, Delhi, 1986

# *India Postcard:*
# *or Why I Make Work in a Racist,*
# *Homophobic Society*

In the canon of world cinema and video, and indeed the written word and other forms of visual representation, there has been a complete silence around the presence of the Indian gay man. One immediate problem, of course, is with definition. *Gay* is a word that does not appear to exist in the vernacular languages of India. The nearest one can come to it is an idea approximating "homosexual relationships"[1] — aside from the usual terms of abuse referring to sodomy, and so on. Furthermore, writing from a British "South Asian" (a term usually truncated to "Asian") perspective about Indian cultural histories can present a problem with boundaries, as the subcontinent is now firmly broken up into separate nation-states. Those of us who live in the West have had the particular experience of redefining and reappraising our cultural position. I, for example, was literally born Indian, became Canadian, moved to London, where I became an ethnic minority, then Asian, then Black, and finally South Asian. I think I would like to return to being simply Indian and a gay man.

Cinema has been the mainstay of Indian popular culture for decades. Bombay musicals dominate regional output and reaffirm the popular mythologies of a secular state and a spoken language that is a hybrid of Hindi and Urdu. The division into India and Pakistan gave rise to a nationalistic drive to enforce each of the languages as the official language of the new state; however, in

India this has met with stiff opposition. Although the country is linguistically divided, the strength of Bombay's commercial cinema continues unabated. Like Hollywood, it has developed its own moral codes: No kissing was allowed, but wanton sexuality was on display. No openly gay characters emerged, but often what was left unsaid created its own unspoken meaning. A campness permeates a number of now-classic films, like *Pakeezah* (1972), *Teesri Kasam* (1966), and *Umrao Jaan* (1981).

I made the *India Postcard* videotape as a greeting, not just from gay men in India to lesbians and gay men in Britain, but specifically also to South Asian lesbians and gay men.[2] The format was a musical with two characters who never meet, except in their subconscious, in Delhi and Bombay. The opening song came from a noir film that describes the villainy of Bombay; the theme was "looking" and cruising, immortalized for us in the song "Chalte Chalte,"[3] whose lyrics literally translate as "walking, I met someone," an event underscored by the whistle of a train, reminding us that sexuality in India is not buried *that* deep under the skin. I felt that by using a cultural device like this, I could get away from the explanatory problematizing of being a cultural minority within a sexual minority, and give some intrinsic pleasure to lesbians and gay men of South Asian origin here in Britain.

One of the most limiting aspects of trying to make work within a foreign dominant culture is constantly having to explain one's references. In short pieces, that means using up most of the duration of the film or tape simply explaining away what it's like to be a double minority, with very little room left for pleasure or developing particular stories. After all, with an Indian population approaching eight hundred million, the general questions can become seriously self-limiting, and in the '90s in Britain, have acquired a sense of déjà vu.

For us South Asian migrants in the West, the pitfalls of a nationalist emphasis on culture can mean that we fall between the cracks. In my view, it's time we reassert our right to be in the center, and demonstrate that as producers of an informed cultural output that forms the link, the basis, of global cultural exchange, we have a voice that goes in both directions. As an Indian gay man living in the West, I take pleasure in my heritage of Indian popular culture, whilst challenging the Eurocentric lesbian and gay world I live within; at the same time, I feel that I have something to contribute to gay men in India as they struggle to assert their own positions.

Originally published in Martha Gever, Pratibha Parmar, and John Greyson, eds., *Queer Looks: Perspectives on Lesbian and Gay Film and Video* (Toronto: Between the Lines, 1993).


Notes

1    In Hindi, the dominant language of North India, *sumlaingik sambandhan*.

2    I made the video for Channel 4's *Out on Tuesday* series in 1989.

3    The song is from the 1972 film *Pakeezah*.

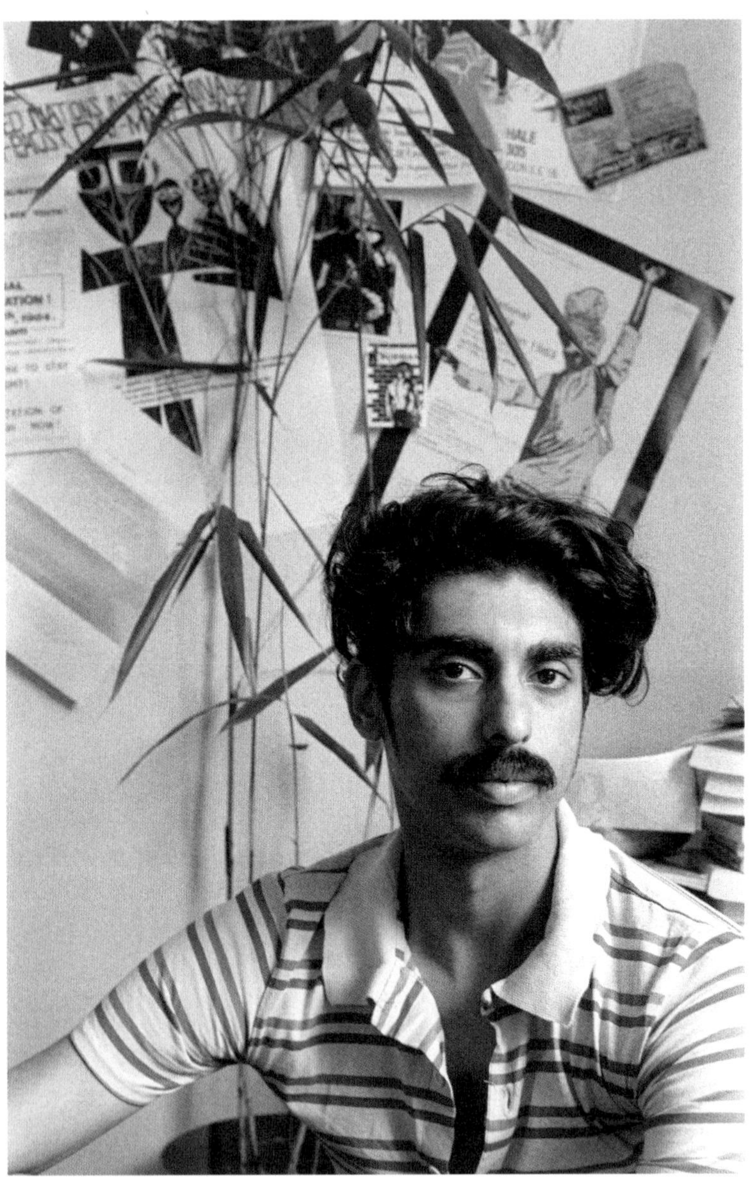

Sunil Gupta, Zahid Dar, London, 1985

# *Black Boys, Shooting Back: The Emergence of a Black Gay Cultural Identity in the UK*

The last decade in the West has seen a growing interest in identity in cultural politics. The avant-garde on the one hand and class issues on the other have been called into question in relation to race politics. Simultaneously, there has been a "coming out of the closet" for lesbian and gay artists dealing with issues of their own identity. London's Institute of Contemporary Arts has hosted at least two conferences around the notion of a "gay sensibility in the arts," and Robert Mapplethorpe's work has come under attack in the US. In Britain, we live with homophobic laws and mindless censorship of so-called "pornography." The Thatcher era coincided with the birth of the Black Arts Movement, during which the hegemony of white art, its history, and institutions have been challenged. Having been the subject of white practice—defined, codified, and catalogued—Black artists have said finally, enough is enough, and have spearheaded demands for autonomous control of their own cultural products and institutions.

An assumption[1] that can be made about the Black Arts Movement is that it was based on an analogy of colonialism, that the Black communities as a colonial labor force were a colonized group within Britain itself. This analogy of the "Third World" within the "First" was partly developed in the US from the varying experiences of people of color. It was introduced to the cultural arena largely through a quote from the Vietnamese filmmaker and theorist Trinh T. Minh-ha: "There is a Third World in every First World, and vice versa." As a concept, it had previously informed the theory of Malcolm X, and subsequently the Black Panthers. In England, membership in the Panthers was held by both African and South Asian activists. From the 1960s on, an increasing number of organizations operated within this African and South Asian coalition. "When we use the term 'Black,' we use it as a political term. It doesn't describe skin colour, it defines our situation here in Britain. We're here as a result of British Imperialism, and our continued oppression in Britain is the result of British racism."[2]

The history of Black[3] photography in the UK is a brief but checkered one. As a documented movement, it's invisible until the early 1980s, when it appeared at the tail end of the metropolitan initiatives by Labour Party–controlled local city governments who sought to create a rainbow coalition between artists and pensioners, races and genders. The radical politics of 1968 in Europe gave way to a Left cultural agenda in the seventies, which brought together visual art and media studies. Photography, art, and politics came together, spawning influential degree courses, galleries, workshops, and publications—Camerawork in London, and *Ten.8* in Birmingham. Grassroots community politics met art photography and were exhibited in London's prestigious Hayward Gallery in an exhibition titled *Three Perspectives on Photography*, curated by Angela Kelly, Paul Hill, and John Tagg. In all the frenetic activity of community groups, writings, and exhibitions, two features were missing: race and homosexuality. There was work done about Britain's racial minorities and the discrimination they faced in housing, employment, and education; but all the work was being produced by white practitioners.

The new radical elite—having fought for a slice of the funding cake, having evolved a rhetoric around critical theory borrowed from literature and film and with its own stars—was still unapproachable by Black practitioners. Even its language was so couched in jargon as to be incomprehensible to the Black

          *BLACK BOYS, SHOOTING BACK*

punter in search of sustenance away from the doggedly white-only, male, and heterosexual mainstream. Looking back, there is an embarrassing feeling that "Oops! They forgot about race."

The early 1980s—into the Thatcher period of national politics, increasing inner-city tensions of race, and emergence of local government bodies like the Greater London Council (GLC) as strident champions of women's rights, lesbian and gay rights, and a host of other marginal groups' rights, which began to fund cultural activities as a strategy to empower these groups and win their political support—eventually saw us at the crossroads of Black photography. A commissioned exhibition was sponsored by the GLC—*Reflections of the Black Experience*, curated by Monika Baker—which was launched at the Brixton Art Gallery. A hundred black-and-white documentary photographs not only provided evidence of Blacks and the variety of their experiences in Britain, but also that there were Black photographers worthy of funding.

A number of issues got simultaneously raised: Why such an exhibition so late in the day? Why the overwhelming use of report-age? How had the gallery system managed to ignore this work for so long? And where were the work and the photographers going onto (since, by then, the demise of the GLC at the hands of Thatcher was a foregone conclusion)? A direct consequence of the exhibition was bringing together a number of Black photogra-phers who began raising these and other questions. The transition of local funding to the Arts Council and the consolidation of a Black arts movement including other art forms to replace the politically impotent notion of "ethnic minority arts" precipitated an overdue policy change—four percent of arts funding was to be spent on Black arts. In terms of photography, this transition sparked a lean period of no funding and the eventual commis-sioning of a research study into Black photographers and what they wanted. Not surprisingly, they wanted darkrooms, project funding, exhibition spaces, and publications that addressed them and their work.

The *Black Experience* exhibition went into limbo when the curator declined to tour it without adequate support. Meanwhile, a simultaneous series of meetings in London took place, coordinated for a while by David A. Bailey, where Black photographers tried to map out a strategy. As time, arguments, and the lack of money took their toll, only a few remained after a couple of years, when the time came to submit a grant application to the Arts Council to form an Association of Black Photographers. This has gone on to become Autograph, a London-based group attempting to serve the needs of the national community. In the interim, a group calling itself D-Max organized a touring exhibition of the same name, and a group of Black women managed to get a one-off magazine out called *Polareyes. Polareyes* was partly symptomatic of the emerging gender-based differences among Black photographers, and D-Max, as an entirely Afro-Caribbean photographers' exhibition, revealed the the problem between cultures under the Black Arts umbrella. D-Max, however, made significant links with the US, in terms of contact with organizers, curators, and photographers, particularly in New York.

Meanwhile, the first National Photography Conference in the UK, held at the University of Salford in 1987, nearly disintegrated over race when the keynote address (by Jo Spence) attempted to sidestep the issue. By the second conference in 1989, Autograph had established itself sufficiently to host Deborah Willis of the Schomburg Center for Research in Black Culture in New York, as well as program a series of workshops addressing in detail issues within the Black photography community. These issues have particularly represented the interests of Black women and Black lesbians and gay men as being the cutting edge of radical cultural politics. No longer were these to be relegated to the fringe.

The lesbian and gay issue has come to the fore because of the general direction of pluralism in the political climate of the left, combined with the threat on the representation of lesbian and gay lives through Clause 28.[4] At the same time, AIDS began to be reported by the British press with an extremely obvious homophobic and racist subtext. Finally, a younger generation of artists, photographers, and filmmakers was coming into its own, and a number of them have had sexuality central to their work. Isaac Julien of Sankofa Film and Video made *The Passion of Remembrance* (1986) and went on to make *Looking for Langston* (1989) and *Young Soul Rebels* (1991); Pratibha Parmar made *Reframing AIDS* (1987) for Converse Pictures, a lesbian and gay video group, going on to make *Flesh and Paper* (1990) and *Khush* (1991) for Channel 4's *Out on Tuesday* program. The radical lesbian and gay magazine *Square Peg* began publishing work by Black photographers like Rotimi Fani-Kayode.

At the same time, throughout the 1980s, the Gay Black Group had met at Marchmont Street in London, providing a different kind of grassroots support and another kind of meeting place for Black cultural practitioners. In fact, toward the end of the GLC, its Ethnic Minority Unit had been persuaded by its lesbian and gay workers to sponsor a day conference on Black lesbians and gays, which was held in Brixton around the time of *Reflections of the Black Experience*. It was not coincidental, then, that the "Black Experiences" issue of *Ten.8* magazine (no. 22) carried a number of pieces about sexuality by lesbians and gay men.

The separatist politics of the 1970s had given way to both a demand for a Black cultural space and a closer and more equal link between the genders and the races. Having won our spaces, the unspoken tensions between the races under the Black umbrella then began to simmer. Funding was inadequate (groups like Autograph exist by the skin of their teeth), and across the art forms Black groups found a lack of skilled administrators and had to take on that onerous task. The rhetoric of employment and training for Blacks in supporting roles nearly sank some groups, and a furious debate now rages whether white skills ought to be enrolled into the promotion of Black arts. The inspiration found in Black American cultural politics lacked the cultural specificity of the South Asian experience, and suspicions were aroused with two US-UK photography shows in quick succession that involved only African/Caribbean artists from the UK. In the context of the US's hegemony in mainstream culture and photography, Blacks in the UK are looking more closely toward their new role as Black Europeans in 1992, when the economic borders of the European Economic Community will come down. Whether "fortress Europe" will be good for us remains to be seen, but it is certainly the area from where comes future funding and the hope of reviving local social democracy.

Lesbian and gay photographers have been with us since the invention of photography, but it is only since the emergence of the politics of representation that they have been allowed to participate in the cultural agenda. Black photographers—always on the defensive, since they inevitably have to speak for the race and fend off attacks from those Black spokespeople who have a vested interest in preserving the Black family as the site of Black experience—have been loath to "come out" in their work. Increasingly in this decade, though, they have been doing so.

Originally published in *Black Boys, Shooting Back* (Perth, Australia: Perth Institute of Contemporary Art/PICA Press, 1992).


Notes

1    Allan deSouza, "An Imperial Legacy," in *Crossing Black Waters* (London: Working Press, 1992).

2    Beverley Bryan, Stella Dadzie, and Suzanne Scafe, *The Heart of the Race: Black Women's Lives in Britain* (London: Virago, 1985), p. 170.

3    *Black* is used here in its 1980s British usage to denote "people of non-European origin" who reside in the UK. The main two groups are African and South Asian, although a number of people of African origin have come from the Caribbean and a number of South Asians have come from Africa.

4    Clause 28, part of a 1988 Act of Parliament limiting the powers of local government, specifically prohibits the "promotion" of homosexuality as a "pretended family relationship." It has raised a whole area of censorship with respect to depicting lesbian and gay lives. Most visual art venues in the UK are subsidized by their town halls.


                                          *BLACK BOYS, SHOOTING BACK*

# *New Internationalism and the New Europe 1992–2005*

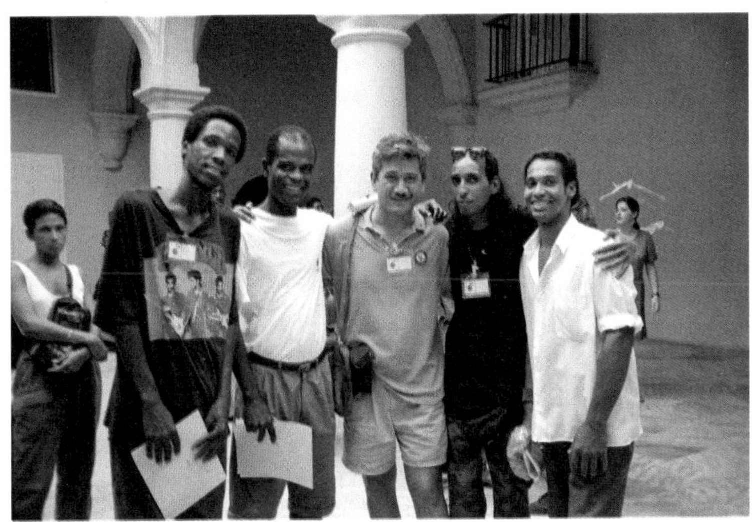

Sunil Gupta (center) and fellow artists at the Havana Biennale, 1995.
Photographer unidentified

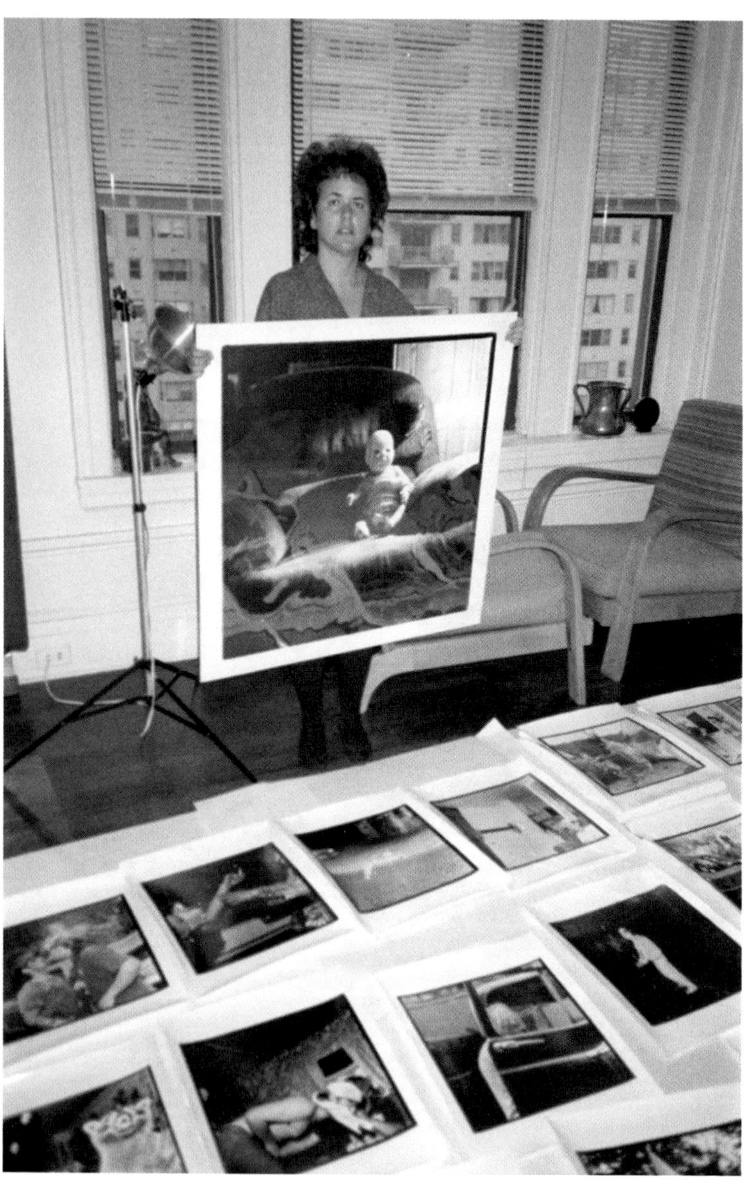

Sunil Gupta, Susan Lipper laying out her book *Grapevine*, New York, 1993

# *Representing the Contemporary: The Artist in the 1990s*

I don't have a paper, so I will tell a story, partly because I perceived this to be a somewhat informal and practical occasion. I was thinking of a good starting point. It's very difficult coming from where I am situated in London. I thought, somewhat arbitrarily, that I would start in the late 1970s, with a report that was commissioned by the Arts Council by Naseem Khan titled *The Arts Britain Ignores*. It's this report that spelled out the notion of "ethnicity" and "ethnic minorities," and it is from then on that the UK's funding bodies began using these terms.

In 1983, I came out of the Royal College of Art, and we staged the first Black students' show there. We invited members of the Greater London Council (GLC), which led to my interaction with town-hall politics. This led me immediately away from my formal and traditional art training into something more like cultural activism. It was in the town hall that Ethnic Minority Units were beginning to be replaced by something called Race Equality Units, and where Anti-Racist Design Committees were being formed. People like myself were being placed on them, and we were finding very quickly that anti-racism was much tougher to spot and define than racism itself.

It was also there that the notion of *Black* became very clearly to do with one's position in relation to power. It was not to do with the color of one's skin. One of the early art exhibitions sponsored by the GLC, *The Colours of Black*, in fact included a whole range of diverse ethnic communities, including the Irish. One of the last GLC shows I was involved in was called *Reflections of the Black Experience.* This was a photography show, and by then, ethnicity had pretty much whittled down to two major ethnic groupings—African Caribbean and South Asian.

Just as that show was going up, Margaret Thatcher was busy closing down the whole of the GLC. So it was too late for us; all these people were brought together and suddenly the institutional body that was supporting us was no longer around! There was a terrible period of being in the wilderness while people regrouped and mounted pressure on the Arts Council of Great Britain (as it was then known). Eventually, a demographic argument that was developed in the last days of the GLC was taken up by the Arts Council, which eventually came out with a policy stating that four percent of its budget would be spent on ethnic minority arts. My particular involvement at that point was to set up an Association of Black Photographers, which came to be known as Autograph. (It's a rather unique grouping. It's still around, I might hasten to add, so it's a relatively successful story, in that it brought together two quite different histories and peoples.) One of the larger strategic initiatives of the GLC was to try and create a building-based institutional home for all Black arts (across the art forms). The Roundhouse in Camden Town was selected as the site. It was very ambitious. It also went down in a rather large blaze of publicity.

In response, the Arts Council distributed the money that was allocated for the Roundhouse to various Black arts organizations. This worked for theater, it worked for film and video, but it didn't work for visual arts, which turned out to be a rather ill-defined group of people who said, "I'm an artist." There wasn't a company to represent art. So the Arts Council initiated a consultancy research project. Two years of meetings took place across four areas of the visual arts, which were exhibitions organization (or curating, as we're calling it here), education, publications, and training issues. A number of us were involved in different levels of these meetings. If you're curious about the results of this, there is a publication called the "red report," which is available from the Arts Council. The result of this study led to Iniva (the Institute of International Visual Arts).

By then, I had begun to organize exhibitions on a freelance basis—partly out of a very selfish motive, finding exhibitions to place my own work in, because nobody else was placing them. It was quite a shock to me to discover everybody wasn't waiting for my work. My projects included *Fabled Territories* (1989), which was very ethno-specific, about South Asians living in the UK; and *Ecstatic Antibodies* (1990–93), a collaboration between myself and Tessa Boffin. This was an idea that got off the ground in a grassroots setting at the London Lesbian and Gay Centre, in a meeting about people interested in AIDS and photography. Tessa and I decided we wanted to do a visual arts show. We thought that all the shows about AIDS up to that point had been about fundraising, and the work wasn't really addressing the issue. We also thought that instead of a catalogue, we would try to do a publication that had some writing.

When Iniva was being planned two and a half years ago, it was decided that rather than set up an institute from scratch and not have any product, running the risk of the Roundhouse fiasco, it would franchise. It decided to offer three franchises. It asked people to tender for these in the name of setting up a program for Iniva, whose legal creation was postponed by two years—two curating and one publishing franchise were given out. Rasheed Araeen of *Third Text* got the publishing franchise, Eddie Chambers and myself got the curating franchises.

For me, the timing was right. I felt I had explored my special-interest areas of being gay and South Asian. I had gone—very unusually—to an auction of Asian art at Sotheby's, and it summed up for me very visibly the problem. I just went to see what the work was. Essentially, it was East and Southeast Asian art, mostly of antiquity. I was very startled to observe (and I must've been very naive) that behind the auctioneer was the board that gave values as people bid. But the currencies on the board were very interesting. US dollars, British pounds, French francs, Japanese yen. They were the G7 currencies, and it struck me that the people who made the work in the countries that the work came from are not involved in the exchange of this work as commodity. That struck me as being fairly dramatic and I thought, I'll join Iniva and try and find a solution, or at least an explanation for how this has come about. I set up a limited company in order to run this franchise. The way we work is entirely based on collaborations. We don't have an exhibiting space, so we look for existing spaces as collaborators. We generate ideas and work intuitively, bringing to it our experiences and knowledge. We try to commission contemporary work. We are not, in the main, looking at collections.

The second project was commissioned for a young Chinese Australian Hong Kong–born artist, Hiram To. He came to London and made a new installation at Camden Art Centre. The third project, which took place in September 1994, was a solo show at the Institute of Contemporary Arts (ICA), Stan Douglas; after much negotiation, they gave us the whole of the ICA, so we were able to show more of his work, including the latest piece, *Evening* (1994).

Earlier this year, I got a phone call from Johannesburg saying, would I come out to an international curators' tour toward a first Johannesburg Biennale. For me, it started an incredible kind of situation, a connection with the place. About thirty-five people came from lots of different countries. Immediately, there was this kind of UN of curators: the white boys from Sydney and New York, the "Third World" lot, and then there was us, who live in the West but are obviously "tinted" (we are in between somewhere) floating backward and forward. We traveled together for two and a half weeks in buses and planes. It was quite intense, and I had meetings every night. I had to make a rule that two white men could not speak one after another, because Tony Bond from

    *REPRESENTING THE CONTEMPORARY*

Sydney and Charles Merriweather from New York would try to take the whole thing over. The biennale also had a very interesting program of trainee curators. South Africa, of course, was so successful with its apartheid that it doesn't have any Black professionals. So they immediately put in place a program of young people coming out of college being hired as trainee curators, and part of the deal of having us out there was that we agreed to host these trainee curators.

I noticed that the interest of Western white curators was discovery. They were determined to find Black art behind every bush, and they were determined to ignore all the white artists. In fact, what South Africa does have in its most developed form are white artists, because they are the only ones that have had that kind of exposure. And it was odd that the Black curators were talking to the white artists, and the white curators didn't want to talk to them. Having the trainees in London was very interesting, because I got to see where I was through their eyes. They went to visit a lot of institutions. They gave me a line, which I'll pass on to you, which is that *they* had apartheid and *we* have equal opportunities. We are equal to be separate in the West. They, in fact, are trying to do something about it, whereas we're not. We're kind of stuck with our status quo. So that was an eye-opener.

Therefore, what's ahead is: *Disrupted Borders* in Ottawa; I'm making a curatorial contribution to the Johannesburg Biennale of three woman artists from England, plus one South African artist; and the Bath Festival next summer — the country they want to look at is South Africa. (It's mainly a music festival, but coincidentally, and I think very fruitfully for my kind of collaborative interests, I can actually now bring South Africa back into England and so, of course, with it we can do our symposiums and publications.) I've also gone back to my roots, and I've become involved in setting up a visual arts festival as part of next year's Pride Festival, which is lesbian and gay pride in London. A new project is a touring exhibition of the work of Fernando Arias, a Colombian artist whom I met at the Havana Biennale, which I'm trying to develop as a collaboration with Contemporary Art Gallery, Vancouver. It will be a new commission. Arias wants to make a new video. The work is all about HIV and AIDS. He'll shoot it in London, and we hope he might edit and complete it in Canada.

I am no longer running a franchise of Iniva's. OVA (Organisation for Visual Arts) is a separate venture with its own policies. Perhaps OVA and Iniva will collaborate where our interests coincide. I feel less inclined to repay the debt to the regions and the history of Black arts in this country. I feel that we have done that enough. A reworking of the international has be the future.

This text was Gupta's presentation at the Critical Practices conference, Tate Gallery, London, 1994.

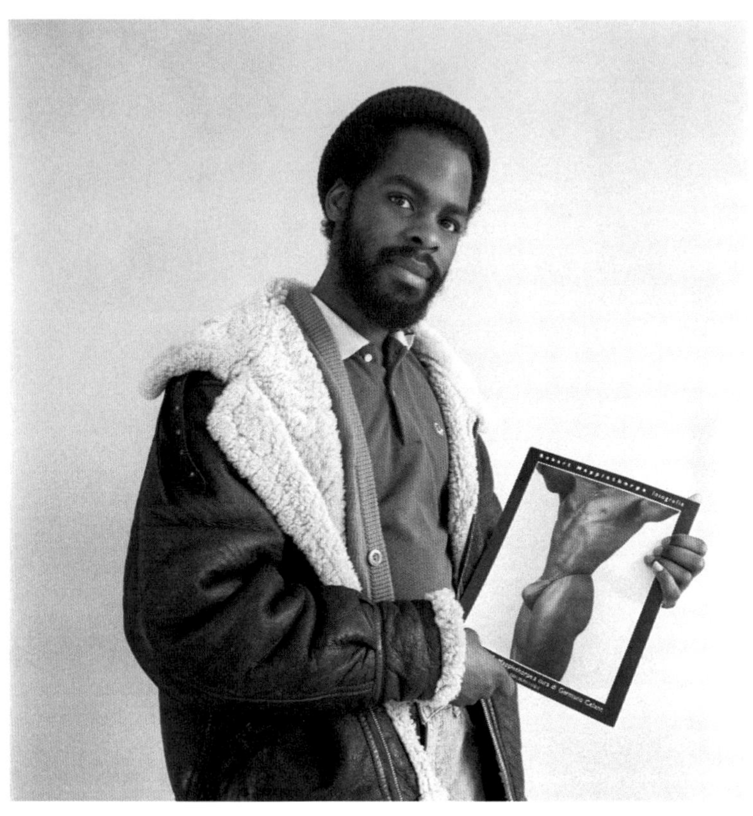


Sunil Gupta, photographer David A. Bailey in Gupta's studio,
Kings Cross, London, 1986

# *Cocks and Other Contradictions:
The Work of Robert Mapplethorpe*

I want to talk about the way Robert Mapplethorpe's homoerotic work positions a critique within a defense of the work, even if the critic is not particularly fond of the images and what they represent. I do not want to discuss the flowers and the portraits for the purposes of this essay. I want to discuss the way I became aware of the work and how the images have reappeared before me over the last twenty years, and how their meanings changed over time. I want to raise certain curiosities about the current show at the Hayward Gallery (London, October 1996). I want to discuss the parallel rise of gay political ideologies which coalesced into the various strategies to fight AIDS in North America and Europe. I want to discuss how all these issues relate to people of color.

Mapplethorpe's most notorious images are focused on black men and their sexuality/sexual organs. The period spanned, the mid-1970s to the mid-1990s, has another parallel, the acceptance of photography as art, particularly in the place where all the above issues were being fought over and where Mapplethorpe lived and worked—New York City. Americans claim to have invented modern photography, and New York is where it found its most influential champions. Not too coincidentally, New York is also seen as the center of the contemporary art world, with the power to settle major issues such as this. Douglas Crimp has written about the cynical appropriation by the art world of photography in *On the Museum's Ruins* (1993).

I am pointing out all these issues since, at the crossroads of all this arrived a lone practitioner, with an attitude toward photography that fit right into modernism, just ripe for canonization. I, too, arrived in New York at about the same time and very soon after my arrival, got diverted from my studies into the photography world of workshops with Lisette Model, and hanging out with dealers who were buying Diane Arbus pictures by the dozen for buyers in Houston during the day and spending their evenings at the Mineshaft. After a while, all this seemed terribly normal. To be trendy, you had to be youngish, gay, male, built like a brick shithouse, and hung like a horse. All kinds of sexual experimentation were both practiced in public places and discussed in fashionable publications. The *Village Voice* sent a woman disguised as a leather man to check out the Mineshaft, and the inevitable experimentation led to the notion of the ultimate sexual trip—terminal sex.

It seemed inevitable that somebody would come and photograph it all. A fellow student of mine at the time, in a photo class, once declared that everything would be photographed—that peculiarly self-satisfied American notion that somehow, technology would solve all our human relationship problems. Mapplethorpe appeared to be seeking this position. He would photograph this underworld and make it explicit. Of course, there is an undeniable contradiction here, as the making explicit of something which, at its core, has desire intersecting with an illicit lust—a hidden expression of what we are capable of doing, if we dare—and rather robs the activities of their personal satisfaction. It's like watching too many porno movies or spending too much time in a sauna—after a while, there is no mythology left, nothing to hang your desire on, just the endlessly repeated nuts and bolts of the action. This is a feature of the Mapplethorpe photos that I find less interesting: on one level, they are mechanical and shed a rather literal light on the human condition; they never seem to catch a moment of desire that might enigmatically engage our attention over a period of time. When it comes to 1970s New York gay scene photos, I much prefer the engaging scenarios of Arthur Tress.

Still, Mapplethorpe gives us *Man in Polyester Suit* (1980), quite simply, a big black dick hanging out of that quintessential American symbol of the working class—the polyester suit. Now, I bet there weren't any pictures of black penises on show in the art world before. I haven't got research on this, but we all know that the art world in the US and Britain likes to retain its lily-white status. Feminists have asked, Where are the great women artists? and blacks have asked, Where are the great black artists? But where indeed are the blacks, even as subject matter? You might think I am exaggerating after "Black Arts" appeared to sweep across the UK in the 1980s, but even today, the visibility count is dreadfully low. It's another sad example of the failure of our equal opportunities policies.

The Mapplethorpe formula of race and gay sex was extremely opportunistic, as it broke across two of the greatest taboos in society and appealed to a metropolitan audience who would be too sophisticated not to notice and dismiss the work as that of an upstart *Drummer* photographer. What's intriguing me is how, on the face of it, such uninteresting photographs came to be canonized in the way that they have been. The style of placing the black men on pedestals and the appeal to racist America's fear of black sexuality has all been done before. Yet Mapplethorpe's pictures have appeared as a novelty. Any number of quite sensible people have rushed to their defense in the anti-censorship debates in America over the fracas engendered by the cancellation of his show at the Corcoran Gallery of Art in Washington, DC.

It seems to me that they have become entangled in the politics of gay liberation. In the post-Stonewall 1970s atmosphere, the ideology of promiscuity became entrenched as a way of flaunting our difference. The occasional and very illegal toilet sexual encounter blossomed into the world of bathhouses and backroom bars. Once you've checked in your identity at the door along with your clothes, your body is free of any social constraints, and it seemed to be an ultimate coming together of politics and pleasure. Unlike some other liberation theologies of the time, this one offered you your cake, and you could eat it too. Naturally, the body had to conform, but that was the largely ignored subtext. You can't shed your skin, so race, and consequently culture, became a barrier.

For me, this binary opposition of black and white seemed to operate to the exclusion of all others. This is what is finally extremely irritating about the Mapplethorpe pictures: they follow the modernist position of showing what is, without referencing complexity. OK! So Robert liked black men, but in the work, the racial issue is tantalizingly raised and then it doesn't go anywhere. Ultimately, it's symbolic of the reductive nature of 1970s gay semiotics. People fashioned specialized sexual roles and advertised them in direct, uncomplicated ways. If you were black or Asian, you had to fit into this rigid straitjacket; you had very few choices. You either went along with the well-hung-black or passive-Asian mythologies, or you withdrew into an exclusive and racially defined subculture.

In Britain, all this has worked in different ways. The black population is much smaller, and half of the Asian population will do its best to ignore questions of sexuality it doesn't like—I doubt if many Asians will be wending their way through the Mapplethorpe work at the Hayward. I came from New York to do degrees at Farnham College and the Royal College of Art and found, to my horror, that attitudes prevailed that were pre-Stonewall. No mention was ever made of any gay practitioners or even a history of the gay subculture: it was left up to me to figure out a canon for myself (Tress, Mapplethorpe, George Platt Lynes, and Minor White). Having discovered it, naturally I defended it in full. Any visual references were, surprisingly, censored. In 1980, Sue Davies gave a lecture to my class and mentioned the Mapplethorpe work, but couldn't show any slides. When Sandy Nairne initially tried to bring the works over to the Institute of Contemporary Arts, they were disbarred by the customs officials, who offered to burn them.

     *COCKS AND OTHER CONTRADICTIONS*

But there was a growing awareness of the pictures. In the 1980s, we discussed them in private, as black gays, and in public in *Ten.8*. I once wrote an article, "Desire and Black Men" [reprinted in this volume, see page 20], which tried to pinpoint the role of the black/Asian male as the subject of homosexual desire. Isaac Julien referenced the pictures in his film *Looking for Langston* (1989). You can't begin a discussion of black gay representation without Mapplethorpe's work, and in that sense, the canonization has worked and the images now function as cultural icons. In Britain, the response has been tremendous given the much smaller base we work from; witness the works of Rotimi Fani-Kayode, Ajamu, and Robert Taylor. It's hard to predict whether the Mapplethorpe pictures will continue to retain their relevance as seminal, pivotal work about black gay men.

At the Hayward opening, we overheard two young women discussing the fist-fucking picture. They couldn't believe the photo was "real" and were trying to convince themselves that it was a fake, a Photoshop phenomenon. Photography remains a tantalizing medium—at once a metaphor for reality, a slice of life, an erotic artifact, and a documentation. In another medium, these images would have lost this appeal—"Are these people really doing what they appear to be doing?" What is annoying about the fist-fucking picture is that it's become disproportionately well known for its artifice, that it tells us very little about the very real dangers to your health involved in this kind of activity, and that it tells us nothing about the participants, since its view is limited to orifice and forearm. Again, a fairly innocuous shot has become fashionable due to censorship. Back then, you could go to a club and see this for real, as you probably can today in London, which is enjoying a 1970s-style revival.

It's difficult to write about Mapplethorpe's work without taking into consideration his untimely death from AIDS. Sometimes seen as a metaphor for the 1970s, much of the work that we recognize now as part of the canon derives from that period and the emerging lesbian and gay sensibilities—a growing awareness that queer subject matter was being appropriated by queer practitioners for a queer audience. That the work is able to cross over into the mainstream at this point is a story of the intersection of a variety of interests, the anti-censorship lobby, the largely closeted gay section of the art world, and the growing public face of homosexuality in the West and its attendant cultural politics.

Originally published in *Portfolio: The Catalogue of Contemporary Photography in Britain* 24 (December 1996).

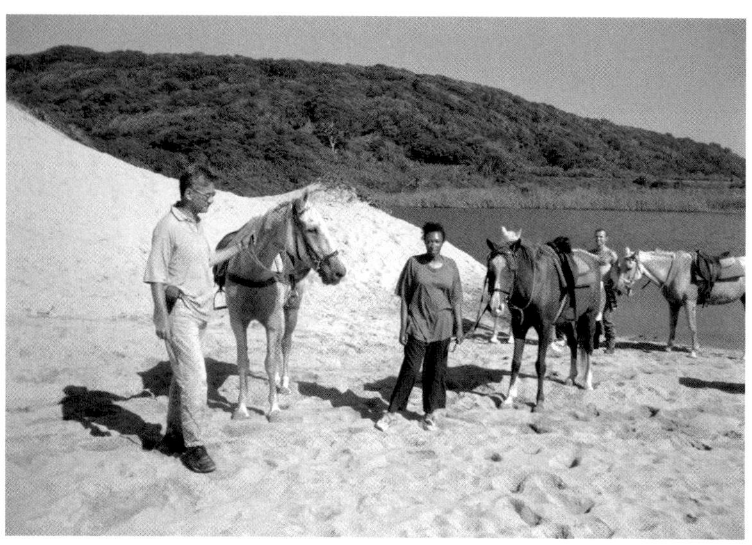

Sunil Gupta, Joy Gregory, and a date Gupta met in a gay bar, Durban, South Africa, 1995. Photographer unidentified

# *Beauty and the Beast: The Work of Joy Gregory*

Joy Gregory is an artist, photographer, and educator who lives and works in South London. Her work is an example of the artist in mid-career whose opportunities have been restricted in particular ways because of gender and race. Straddling the conundrum between truth and beauty on the one hand and race and gender politics on the other, it has not been easy for her work to gain the attention it might have had she chosen either a more polemical route or foregone cultural politics altogether in favor of a more restricted formal practice.

From her work's student origins at the Royal College of Art's studios, it has depicted fragments and layers of herself. In some senses, the work started out with the classic, stereotypical "feminine" qualities of soft contours, architectural interiors as stand-ins for the body and self-portraiture. Even the still lifes and flower pictures were more in the photography tradition of Olivia Parker's Polaroids rather than the male traditions of Robert Mapplethorpe. They are again metaphors for body interiors rather than observed objective views of exterior sexualized organs. There was evidence everywhere that the artist was a woman, indeed a black woman.

Her arrival in the art world, at that particular moment in the 1980s—after the initial teething problems of the Black Arts Movement—meant that at least some of the groundwork had been laid. Coming to London from Manchester meant that Gregory had avoided the personal history of an involvement with the Greater London Council, whose experiments in cultural politics left their mark on the generation of local artists that went on to define Black Arts.

Her work managed to avoid the pitfalls of polemical references that signaled so much of the work produced at the time. Instead, she concentrated on craft and technique. Reworking nineteenth-century processes, she evolved a position that has found her a unique niche as a black woman with abilities and references that reach out into the wider white world and its history of arts and crafts. To a degree, this has alienated her from the purists of whatever color, who seek an artistic expression that parrots equal opportunities policies; yet, inevitably, this is also her burden. This is the Beast of Race politics that she finds herself trapped within.

The work commissioned by Autograph for the *Autoportraits* exhibition (Camerawork, London, 1990) was a series of stark black-and-white confrontational pictures that focused on her upper body and face. Here, she was beginning to get away from the layering and softer treatment toward something more *in-your-face*, more along the lines of the demands being made by the Beast. Examples of this kind of angry rhetorical work is a mainstay of identity politics. It particularly calls on the camera's ability to draw accurate representations of that which is feared most—a rendering of skin tone.

But, skin is that most interesting of organs, in that it is in touch with both the inside and the outside worlds. The glamorized self that was rendered here has given way to *Objects of Beauty* (Sometime/s, London, and Johannesburg Biennale, 1995, and touring), where the objects themselves are now the focus of attention. Beauty, for Gregory, is also under investigation, and truth remains subjective. "Black is beautiful," said Angela Davis and the Black Panthers in the 1960s, and *Beauty* is a magazine that might be bought by black women as their guide to glamour and the right products to be used. Gregory is negotiating a delicate path between the political demands of making the Black body visible and desirable, and subverting the conventions of beauty as expressed by the fashion industry. Her work finds the slippages in that the same images can be used as both rallying cries for Black women's identity as well as illustrations for magazine work. That they also function as art and are collected by museums is no small achievement.

In an international context, particularly in Africa, Gregory found a much more sympathetic audience. In Africa, there appear to be few problematics about race and identity in relation to her work. The work is unquestionably located in UK practice, so her Britishness is not called into question, and her skin color is no problem. As an educator, she is in great demand. In South Africa, where black professionals are few and far between, a black woman with a good grasp of technical and aesthetic skills was treasured. Here, the Beast is laid to rest, in a land where Zulu meets Xhosa, where even the seemingly all-powerful Greco-Roman traditions are subverted to indigenous needs.

It's in the Diaspora residents of the West that the Beast reigns supreme. At a discussion at 198 Gallery in Brixton in 1995, Gregory was again accused by another black woman of being a "black white woman" because she spoke the language of the white majority. She was being victimized by her own successes in the system. Arguably, she had allowed that by participating in an all-Black series of shows, by entering the belly of the Beast.

Floating, unanchored, to tradition is the Beast we all confront as citizens of a nation whose history has been to denude us of our own traditions. Do we now grasp postmodernity with both hands as the theoretical savior of our souls? Borrowing references from any tradition we choose? Do we have access to all? Or to none?

What, then, of the art itself? Working in the secular traditions of the West, which are spreading round the world along with Western capitalism, Gregory is best appreciated in the context of the international. An art that is engaged with contemporary concerns which draws viewers in by using aesthetic pleasure to trigger a response. A practice that is rooted in her historical context as a South London black woman.

The tool that she has chosen to fight the Beast is Beauty. What better allegory to grasp and subvert than this fairy tale known to all in the West and now spread far and wide as a Disney vehicle. For all of its rounded contours and feminine gaze, Gregory's works are calling attention to an urgent need, to redefine the cultural significance of the color of skin. That organ with which we confront the outside world, which we cannot shed and which protects our interiors from the onslaught of the world. It is not a Beast that will be easily laid to rest, but at least Gregory's work helps us to peel back the layers and understand its mechanisms, using the traditions of her time and place—using Beauty to reveal a truth.

Originally published in *Joy Gregory: Monograph* (London: Autograph, 1995).

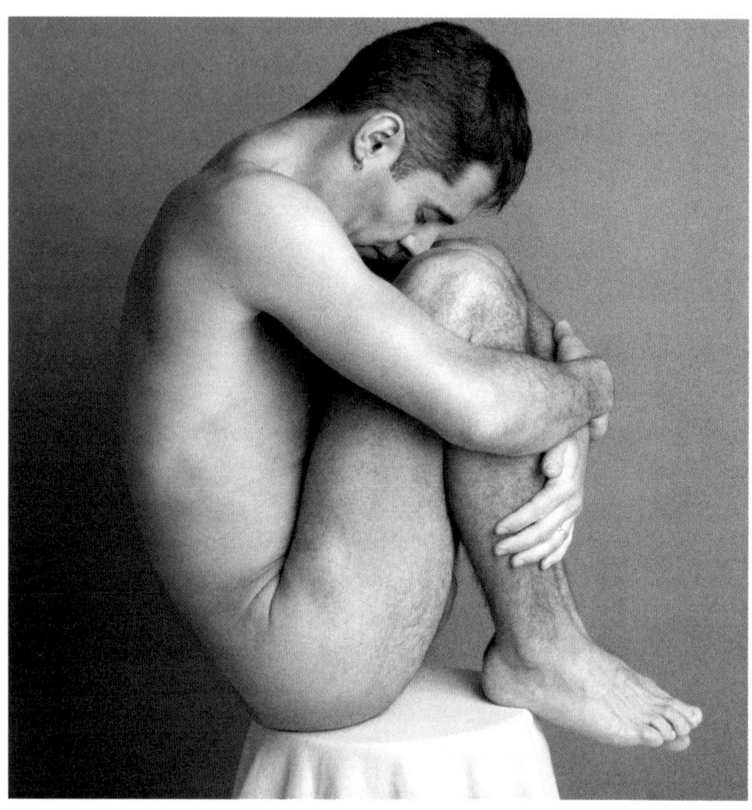

Sunil Gupta, *The Body Positive*, an unpublished project originally made for Michael Petry's curation of the back of a porn store, Kings Cross, London, 2004

# *On Visual Arts and AIDS*

There is a wealth of cultural production embedded in the vast quantities of material produced as a response to HIV/AIDS. This has and is occurring around the globe. The way in which we, as audience, most frequently seem to encounter it is in the form of educational matter, whether in some form of advertising media or in the more popular form of printed matter. Educators and activists have to relay the ever-evolving clinical news into a form that is easily understood by their audiences. In a way, they have to rely on some sort of cultural production to interpret their message.

To a certain extent, we are all familiar with and accept the material representation of HIV/AIDS as a populist strategy. The burden of this representation seems to have fallen on the media-based arts of film, video, and photography. While there has been a shift away, in the West, from the melodramatic media coverage of AIDS in the mainstream press of the 1980s, the coverage of the epidemic in non-Western countries remains in the "victim" mold, perhaps justified by fundraising strategies. In some places, like India, there are still no campaigning images to be seen and certainly no art shows. Curious, in a country where the visual image is everywhere and where it plays a quite central role in its theology. In the UK, people of color suffer from this invisibility factor, except occasionally as victims, a situation challenged only by the campaigning leaflets and postcards produced by NAZ Project London and GMFA, which are specifically targeted at black and minority communities.

This becomes more problematic when fine art invokes the politics of representation. Artistic practices sitting somewhere on the continuum between universal human truths and individual experience have to pose questions. In this way, they are almost opposed to the tactics of the educators, even though they might borrow their forms of expression. One might wonder what fine art has to do with life-threatening epidemics. The American AIDS activist and author Douglas Crimp has written, "Art does have the power to save lives, and it is this very power that must be recognized, fostered, and supported in every way possible." But he adds, "if we are to do this, we will have to abandon the idealist conception of art." By that, he was referring to the way the art world seems to live in its own ivory tower, quite divorced from popular culture. He was calling for a radical change, in which art institutions think about art calling for their support.

To a certain extent, this did happen in New York, arguably the cultural capital of the world, and also a city where the arts were affected quite severely by the epidemic. Almost two decades later, there is the cultural legacy of ACT UP (the AIDS Coalition to Unleash Power), the red ribbon, major artworks that invoked HIV/AIDS, and the tragic loss of some of the cutting-edge visual artists of their time, such as Keith Haring and Félix González-Torres. Visual AIDS continues to flourish as an organization that archives and promotes the work of artists with HIV.

The same cannot be said of the UK. At the end of the 1980s, some colleagues and myself took on the Arts Council and the visual arts galleries to give us space to put on shows that questioned our understanding of HIV issues. We thought we were at the beginning of some movement for radical change here. But it hasn't turned out like that. There were no dramatic Day Without Art events here, and if there were, they were buried in the media.

  

The mainstream art world here has turned away from issue-based activist art, to the extent that even artists of color would not want to foreground their race, as it might be seen as a handicap in their careers.

But it might be that the current obsession with minor celebrities that is plaguing us here, in the UK, will run out of steam. Decibel, an Arts Council initiative, is trying to bring race back into the agenda; and next summer, the New Art Gallery of Walsall will stage an important show looking into the way gay experiences have been obliterated from art history. These are some hopeful signs that the British art world is again willing to engage with AIDS and other issues.

Originally published in *Raseneh Khaberie* (NAZ Project London Newsletter), Issue 18, Winter 2004.

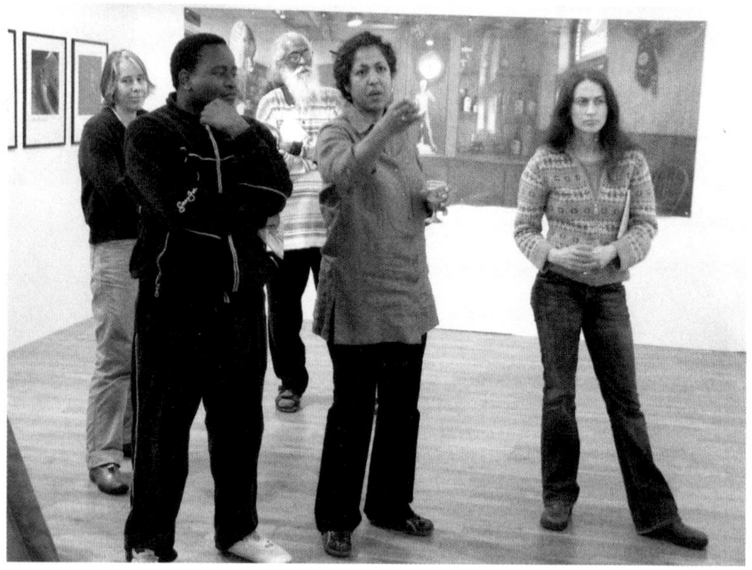

Sunil Gupta, Roshini Kempadoo explains her work, as her father and Emily Andersen look on, City Art Gallery, Leicester, UK, 2004

# *Shades of Black*

In April 2001, when the conference that *Shades of Black: Assembling Black Arts in 1980s Britain* is based on was held at Duke University, I was unable to attend, so I am very pleased that the discourses that took place are going to be made available in print. Together with the additional papers and added bonuses of the timeline and extended bibliography, the book is a valuable and rare resource on a period that shaped many of our lives here in London. Its impact was felt far and wide, at other urban centers in the UK and also overseas, particularly in the English-speaking world.

It's also fitting that the impetus should come from two of the editors, David A. Bailey and Sonia Boyce, who were jointly managing the African and Asian Visual Arts Archive (AAVAA) at the University of East London at the time. AAVAA is the repository of what used to be called Black Arts, from a time when very little documentation existed or was saved. So there are few historical records available to researchers now. AAVAA was originally the personal slide library of Eddie Chambers, who went around photographing the various shows, and frequently these were the only visual records of the events.

What wasn't recorded were the raucous meetings that preceded and accompanied many of these exhibitions and events. I entered this world on graduation from the Royal College of Art (RCA) in

1983. A bunch of us organized the first ever Black student show in a separate room given to us by the college around the time the graduation shows were on. We were visited by representatives of the Greater London Council's Ethnic Minority Unit, and they seemed very pleased to find us. I think they were pleased to find a collection of articulate arts graduates who were willing to make a case for color. The next thing I know, I was diverted from my own brilliant art career into town-hall politics. For me, the relationship between local politics and cultural producers was key to the whole Black Arts idea. Although my own experience of it was largely limited to the visual arts and, particularly, to photography as a medium.

I have been in very traditional British art schools, where art was taught for art's sake alone which, while very good for the development of technique and self-confidence in dealing with the material issues of making things, was quite indifferent to the larger world outside—one that we invited in on that fateful day to our opening. Very shortly after, I wasn't doing the rounds of commercial art galleries but walking the hallowed halls of County Hall, now ironically the home of Charles Saatchi's latest gallery space. But just as I was beginning to acquire new skills and an understanding of cultural politics, Margaret Thatcher was busy closing the place down. Suddenly, having drawn together as a diverse group of visual artists and photographers, we saw the demise of our only institutional backer. There was an awkward pause before we realized that we would have to target the major national funding body in the arts, the Arts Council of England (as it is now called).

While *Shades of Black* is giving voice to a number of key theorists, critics, and practitioners of the period, I find it is a little short on the role of local government in the fostering of the movement, because at the time, it certainly wasn't happening in the colleges. There weren't many Black students in the arts and definitely no Black teachers. My own teachers, I recall, viewed the British Raj as a good thing for India, my place of birth. Photography, as I studied it, seemed to have been born in Europe in the nineteenth century, and then developed as a modern artform in the US. There was never a mention of the work done elsewhere in the five years of higher education I undertook in Britain at the time. In the end, I had to invent my own cultural history.

Naseem Khan's chapter in the book is the only one that addresses the role of the funders and policy-makers. She points out, rightly, that there was a lot of clamor at the time for new policies as the artists were there doing things. Looking back, she asserts correctly, I think, that the policy-makers failed us, because the situation has scarcely changed. However, the demographics have shifted a great deal. London is now around thirty percent non-white and this proportion is set to grow. In the face of this, there is hardly any provision for this growing segment of the population. Yet the funders continue to churn out more policies and ring-fence yet more money; one wonders where it is all going to, as it seems to have hardly any effect at all.

Lubaina Himid's piece in the book is a highly entertaining and slightly tongue-in-cheek one about the inner workings of the period. About who got the shows and how they went about it. It's not often that these things get said in public. That things didn't happen in some kind of glow of unanimity. There were very real and fought-over differences that frequently got covered over in the face of the larger battle being waged with the mainstream arts sector and the funding bodies. Women, though, did manage to break away on more than one occasion. They had shows of their own, and Himid managed her own gallery space for a while. Like all the rest of the activity, there is little concrete to show for it now. Nearly all the Turner Prize nominees have been men so far: Isaac Julien, Chris Ofili, Steve McQueen, Yinka Shonibare and, of course, Anish Kapoor.

Kapoor is a sore point, as he made a big issue of not wanting to be included in *The Other Story* (1989), Rasheed Araeen's groundbreaking Black arts show at the Hayward Gallery, and thus raised the issue of a certain divisiveness in the ranks. The

Turner Prize could almost be read as his reward from the British art establishment. It's interesting that, although several Black nominees for government merit awards like the OBE (Order of the British Empire) have turned these down, Black artists have never turned down the Turner Prize on the grounds that it is administered by a racist institution.

Throughout the 1990s, during the meteoric rise of the YBA (Young British Artists) stars, to raise the issue of "Black" became very unfashionable. The inclusion of a few Black artists on the Turner short lists seemed to be enough for many people that the art world was no longer racist. Of course, that is not the case, as we can see the policy-makers once again floundering in the face of multiculturalism, now reborn as "diversity." Take an institution like London's Southbank Centre—out of two thousand employees, only about two hundred might be Black or Indian, nearly all are in catering or security, and only one Indian is in management (as an accountant).

I've been an arts manager for twenty years as a means of support, but I can't get a job other than in a Black arts center; although my training took place in a perfectly bona fide British institution, the RCA, I'm not allowed to have a curatorial opinion on white art history. Meanwhile, there are no Black arts centers, so there are no jobs for either me or all these Black arts trainees that have been churned out by various failed multicultural policies. People often say it's hard to pinpoint racism, and I always point out that it's about jobs in the end.

So did the Black Arts Movement in 1980s Britain matter in the end? As a person with a vested interest, I would like to think that it did. And *Shades of Black* is a timely reminder as our funders try and figure out what's next, and our colleges grapple with the latest shifting trends. It's also coming at a time when, finally, there will be a concrete legacy, literally. Iniva (the Institute of International Visual Arts) and Autograph (Association of Black Photographers), the two organizations which sprang from roots in the 1980s, have come together to build a new space to house their activity and showcase art. The building project is called Rivington Place, and as one of their ambassadors, I can say that it is looking very likely that it is going to happen this time.*

But what about theory? I had an encounter during the Art after Modernism conference in Toronto a couple of years back with Irit Rogoff, who runs the new Visual Cultures department at Goldsmiths College in London. In the new millennium and the new internationalism, race doesn't matter anymore. Work is somehow devoid of these peculiarities of cultural context. But I tend to agree with Rasheed Araeen's question in *Shades of Black*: why should white experience stand in for the universal? Which seems to be the undercurrent of the theorists.

Stuart Hall argues the case brilliantly for Black Arts, that it unleashed a huge hidden potential. That this was not taken up by the art world to the extent that it took up the case of the YBAs that followed it is a troubling political question for Britain. As for me, I've had enough after twenty years of broken promises and false starts, and as I conferred with Hall in a private conversation last year, I have started a small process to repatriate myself to India, a place that has the largeness of culture to accommodate difference to a much greater degree than I have witnessed in the West—something that seems to have been a well-kept secret in the annals of art historical discourse over here in the UK.

Originally published in *FUSE* magazine, Toronto, February 2005.

*Editor's note: Gupta is here referring to a venture by the Greater London Council in 1985 to establish a dedicated building for Black arts at the Roundhouse, Camden Town, London, which stalled in controversy in 1986, as discussed in "Representing the Contemporary: The Artist in the 1990s," reprinted in this volume (see page 54).

# *Queer Delhi*
# *2005–2013*

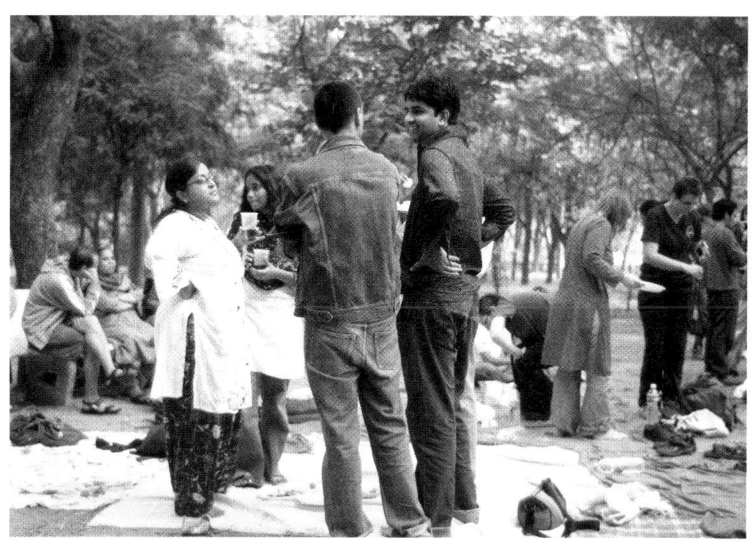

Sunil Gupta, Nigah, a queer activist group, having a picnic in Delhi, 2008

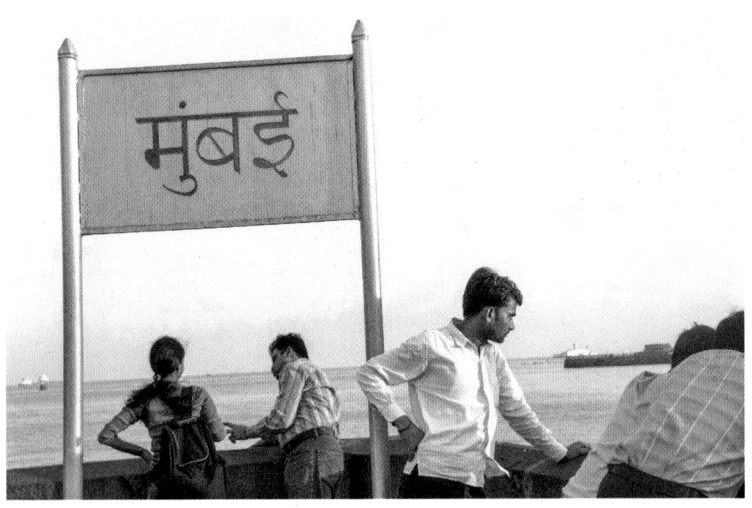


Sunil Gupta, At the Gateway of India, Mumbai, published with the *Mail Today* column "City of Dreams," 2006

# *Pride and Prejudice:*
# *The* Mail Today *Columns*

## A RETURN FROM EXILE

*Exiles.* Yes, that's what I called my photo art project in the 1980s that took a close personal look at gay life in Delhi. Well, what passed for gay life, at any rate. It wasn't a very happy scene. A few, like me, found ourselves outside the country and chose to remain there. Those that were here made the best of it by remaining as silent and invisible as possible.

The nineties came and went. I became part of the great Indian Diaspora. To distance myself from it, I focused my research and work on other parts of the world: Australia, South Africa, Malaysia. Home became London, that melting pot of Diasporas. Gays there came in all shades of skin tone and ethnic origin.

At the turn of the millennium, the news from Delhi became more positive. Gay life was making itself felt, and things were getting better. Wouldn't I like to show my work here? The question was asked. I made another body of work seeking to locate the geography of homelands. There was Canada, where my parents had migrated to; there was New York, where I had gone to finally escape from them; then there was London, what seemed like my final resting place. But, inescapably, there was Delhi.

Here, where I was born and bred. Some of whose central neighborhoods are etched in my memory. Nizamuddin, which was home, and Humayun's Tomb, which was a fantastic playground.

In 2004, I finally got to show all this work at the India Habitat Centre's art gallery and met a wide variety of people. One of whom laid a healing hand on my shoulder. In response, I decided to move back here. To become part of the changing face of Delhi. And to reconnect with a long-lost gay childhood.

–May 17, 2006.


## RELATIVE VALUES

It's training day for the immigration officer at Indira Gandhi International Airport. It's taking twice as long. "What's your father's name?" comes the obligatory question. "Shri Ram," I say. He looks at me long and hard. I start to feel a little guilty—how could a Shri Ram have produced a queer son? I wonder if he can tell? But no, we're virtual cousins, he's from a similar caste background, all is well, and I'm free to catch the flight to London.

These flights are long and boring. I amuse myself by trying to engage the attention of the very handsome young steward strapped in his seat facing me. But he's Indian and very shy. I suppose I shouldn't assume every male flight attendant is gay. I wonder if he has a secret life and will hit some of the more sleazy clubs that night in London.

Terminal 3 at Heathrow is remarkably empty. I'm out of there in record time. No sign of anyone to greet me. My ex-lover calls. He's on his way, how did I manage to get out so quickly? I agree to meet him outside. It's raining, naturally, and it's a shock to go from forty-five to fifteen degrees Celsius. I'm hoping the Delhi heat will tide over my insides in this cold and grey city.

Finally, we're home. One over-excited dog, one surviving parent, one recently divorced sister, and one niece. I'm in the bosom of my family. The signs don't look good; no family ensemble at the airport and no favorite food on the table. The next two weeks are going to be a long haul. Living within the family means no cruising long hours in London's gay scene. But I had planned my escape. I have an internet date for the following night!

–May 24, 2006.

## THE END OF MARRIAGE

Rain. It hasn't stopped the whole time I've been here. After a while, a kind of melancholia sets in. I tried to hold on to the heat of Delhi as long as possible. But, now I've succumbed to cloudy skies and sniffles. Conversations this week in London have centered on two spectacular divorce settlements. Heterosexual marriage seems to be over.

Meanwhile, gay couples are rushing to the "altar." Well, not quite the altar, as these are not called marriages. In their usual display of political sleight of hand, the British decided not to call these unions a "marriage," and thus took the wind out of the sails of the opposition.

But I am perplexed as to how this came about. The Gay Liberation Front was born at the London School of Economics in the early 1970s. Marriage and property, it proclaimed, are the twin pillars of patriarchy that oppress both women and men.

Queer women and men came out and were proud, not ashamed anymore, to be different. But it seems, in time, the "straight-acting" gay appeared on the scene, embarrassed by the more flamboyant queens. They, who were never at the forefront of the queer street, who never got their heads bashed in, suddenly ascended to set the agenda of appeasement.

Gay men are just like everyone else, wanting the right to marry and settle down. Men in suits appeared and formed lobbying organizations. We should marry, buy property, and raise children, they said.

It's not popular to say that one is anti–gay marriage, not wishing to be aligned with the religious right. But are we chasing after an institution that has lost its meaning even in the heterosexual world? Under these grey skies, there is a sadness for some lost ideals.

–May 31, 2006.

## A LAYING ON OF HANDS

I've agreed to meet someone via the e-list. Seeing as I didn't get laid in London despite two Gaydar dates, this is the next best thing. I'm beginning to feel guilty about my fleeting, sexless visits to the gay hedonistic capitals of the West. In a curious reversal, London is dominated now by the baggage of ex-lovers and family, and Delhi is where I am free.

We're meeting in my local Barista in the early evening. I'm trying not to become too frazzled by domestic water and power issues, trying to maintain my cool, ditch my cold, and fight off jet lag. If we can meet by 6 as planned, I'll be fine. However, there are SMSs and phone calls to the contrary: Can we meet later? Can we meet another day?

This is not looking good. Why did I agree to this? I've thought about this encounter for nine hours on a plane. If it's not going to happen this evening, it's not going to happen at all. I'm trying not to feel irritated by gay Delhi's latest closet of the internet and mobile phone. Finally by 9, I'm unwisely pushing for us to meet at home, not fancying another pointless visit to Barista in my increasingly jet-lagged state.

The bell rings. He's not what I expected at all. At least he's not in his twenties. We talk for a longer time than usual. I find out that, like me, he's also been recently dumped, and we're both in an emotional free fall. I was expecting to offer him support, but I think he might offer me some in return. He's struck a chord in me. It's what they call chemistry. This is not just any old meeting, I've met someone!

–June 7, 2006.

"Go to Bombay." That's what everyone has said to me. It's got a better gay life, a better art scene.

She rang up and asked, would I like to show three pictures in her summer salon? She's sold one of the pictures before the opening. That convinces me to go. Just for one night.

All too quickly, I'm there. Within minutes, my clothes are sticking to me. I'm not going to look cool by the time the opening starts.

The gallery is all the way down by the Taj. I escape briefly to the Gateway. It's too early in the evening. The place is swarming with straight couples. But there are single men arriving, mingling with the crowd. I want to linger, to see how things develop, but I can't. I have to be at the gallery. I make a few pictures and head back to encounter the local art world.

I'm introduced to a potential one-night stand. He's young and pretty, but his attention is wandering every couple of minutes. No good. Talk to an older and more likely candidate. He makes yachts, not a very gay occupation, plus his wife is holding court. Doesn't look promising, but then it's India and anything is possible.

On the plane back to Delhi, the woman beside me strikes up a conversation. I confess to being artistic, unmarried with three unfulfilled relationships behind me. But I avoid mentioning their gender. She's married with a young child but enjoys a corporate career. By now she's giving me her number, and then it hits me that I'm being picked up! I wonder whether it's worth telling her I'm gay but decide that it's a short plane ride, so why not entertain her fantasies? She has to have her dreams as well.

–June 14, 2006.

Sex. How we all obsess about it. No one seems to be getting enough. At least, not of the right kind. We've dressed it up in so many flavors. Given it national characteristics, like culinary curiosities. In India, it's not done, we're told.

At puberty, I developed a problem of nocturnal emissions, which led to a trip to the doctor in Connaught Place. Following an acutely embarrassing examination of my penis, all was declared normal and I was packed off with a set of relieved parents. Little did we suspect what lay ahead.

The subject of my sexuality was officially closed in the family. I experimented by storing the results of my consciously induced daytime emissions in a Pond's cold cream jar. An appeasement to the Gods. However, not a good idea at the height of a Delhi summer.

Moving on to the oral stage, still uninformed about consequences, it came as a huge surprise that someone would use me as a cold cream jar.

Two years ago, I fell in love with the most beautiful Delhi man I had ever met. Within a year it was over, unconsummated. He had found his Meera; he didn't need sex, meaning me, anymore.

Last Saturday night I decided, enough was enough. I head out on the town. No luck, club shuts and we're back out on the road. I see a man on a motorbike. He'll do. I never chose celibacy. My friends hang out encouragingly. Back home, he just lies there. No one's taught him anything. I administer my oral skills. He blows in minutes. Doesn't make a move toward me. The night is over.

Will someone decriminalize the act? Spread basic information and bring spontaneity and fun back into our Indian sex lives?

–June 21, 2006.

Pride. That word now shorn of its gay prefix in these times of floating identities. Some marketing hack decided that the short list of identifiable sexualities might be too much of a mouthful. However, it was celebrated at the end of June across the world, even in India with a small march in Kolkata.

London has announced crowds of up to half a million people. In Delhi some of us marked it by exchanging a message or two. All that is allowed. The illegality of it, the blanket social approbation. People living under such extreme conditions start behaving in extreme ways. How to negotiate simple acts such as meeting another human being, how to develop a more fulfilling sex life, an emotional life, a spiritual life. Altogether a more whole and humane existence.

Instead, we have the spectacle of furtive, fleeting meetings. People only sticking around long enough to find out if you are willing to take it or give it. The whole act of love reduced to simple equations of giver and taker. Intimacy, well, there is no room for that. And the possibility of sharing a life. That seems beyond the realm of possibility.

So why is Indian society so prejudiced and basically so ignorant? It's hard to believe that things have always been this way. Whenever our voices are raised, we're told to shut up. It's un-Indian or something. Now why would it be un-Indian to live in blissful ignorance? Wouldn't it make more sense to make oneself more aware?

Before I returned to Delhi, I was told that things had become cool over the last thirty years. I can't see any evidence of that. It seems that the old prejudices are all intact. With the vast majority of people unable to act and the leadership still muffled.

However, yesterday there was a press conference at which many voices were heard in support of removing the anti-sodomy law, even while acknowledging that rampant prejudice still exists against homosexuality. Tonight, there is going to be a television program during which Vikram Seth will announce his homosexuality in person. We need such pillars of our society to come out. It makes an enormous positive impact on the self-image of millions of gay people in this country.

Then, perhaps the courts will decide to remove the law. That will mark a beginning from where gay people can regain their self-worth and pride, their human rights as contributing citizens of this society.

–September 17, 2006.

Editor's note: Gupta wrote these columns for *Mail Today*, New Delhi, throughout the summer of 2006. The newspaper then discontinued his columns, deeming them too sexually explicit.

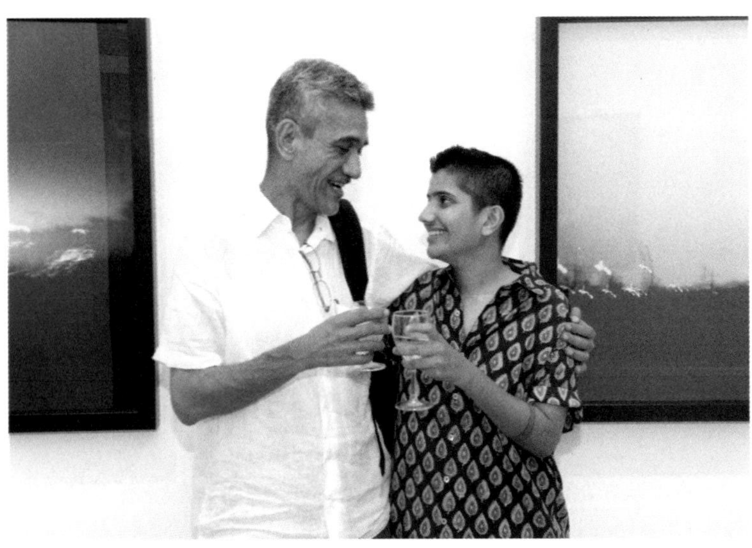

Sunil Gupta and Tejal Shah at their group exhibition at Galerie Mirchandani + Steinruecke, Bombay, 2007. Photographer unidentified

# Indian Art and Alternate Sexuality

Given the prevailing norms of heterosexual family units based on an economic need to guarantee the transition of property, any deviation might be thought of as an alternative. Art practices throughout history and across the world have sought to challenge these prevalent myths of normality. In the latter half of the twentieth century, some of these practices became allied to larger social movements and, in the West, began to be named. There is a trajectory that can be traced from the Civil Rights Movement in the US, through the women's movement and the ensuing struggles for the emancipation of all kinds of sexualities. Artistic production followed and occasionally led—sometimes as propaganda, and sometimes to pose difficult questions.

Now, in the twenty-first century, both what is Indian and what an alternative sexuality might be are under scrutiny. Within India itself, there has been the recent history of exhibiting increasingly explicit art. Twenty-five years ago, some of these shows might not have been able to see the light of day. But somewhere between the work of Bhupen Khakhar and Tejal Shah, a quiet revolution has taken place, at least in the possibility of exhibition. Khakhar's paintings that include imagery of love and desire between two men have become internationally famous. Shah is a young emerging artist whose video installations question notions of contemporary queer identity in India.

I have largely used photography and, to some extent, video in my own work. In the 1980s, I felt unable to work and exhibit in this way in India and made a seminal work called *Exiles*, which tried to visualize how gay men had been excluded from Indian society. It also discouraged me from returning to live here. Now, however, the social climate appears to have changed. In 2004, Radhika Singh curated a show in Delhi which dealt with my experiences of queer sexualities. The largely positive response to that show has encouraged me to move my practice back here.

As more pressure is brought to bear by artists on our sometimes very conservative curators and other custodians of culture, there will be an opening up of a wider critical debate among gallery audiences and, eventually, the general public around notions of Indian sexual identity.

Originally published in New Delhi, 2005.

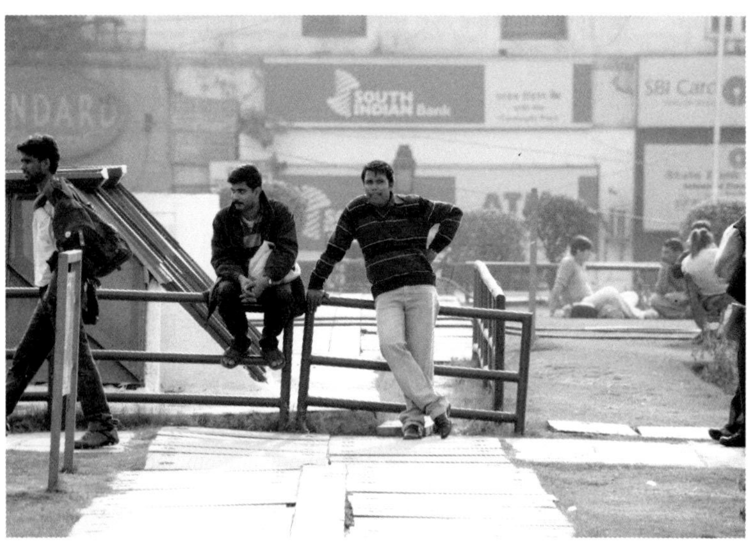

Sunil Gupta, Above Palika Bazaar, a gay cruising site for many years, Delhi, 2008

# *Queering the Indian Street*

Finally, that season is upon us when the weather is ideal for the outdoors in Delhi. But where can we go in this city of ours? In spite of the plethora of neighborhoods serving every kind of need, there are none that are obviously lesbian or gay. On the other hand, our streets are full of loitering men, so it may seem like a homosocial paradise, at least for gay men. However, they present more a threat than an invitation. The street is clearly unsafe for women in general and, I would add, for feminine men. The issue revolves around thwarted masculinities and male posturing. Everything feminine is subject to verbal abuse and physical attack.

Out of the many varied struggles for human rights, the lesbian and gay one has been particularly identified with actual streets. Christopher Street in New York is seen as the birthplace of gay liberation, and the Castro District in San Francisco as the place that developed a modern gay identity. Today, you can't be living in a "world-class city," as the punters like to call them, unless you can point to a gay street in your town, like Old Compton Street in London's Soho.

Before you rush to tell me that this is all happening solely in the "developed" world, let's remind ourselves that Mexico City has a well-developed queer neighborhood. So what is stopping us here, in Delhi, from carving out a space? After all, the arguments for the implementation of rights have been laid out and well understood. Never before has it been as cool as it is nowadays to be lesbian and gay. So where is Delhi's gay geography?

For the urban middle classes, it's in South Delhi, but you leave your sexuality at home when you step outside to visit the market. It took the extreme act of the Pushkin murder to have this privacy invaded by the media a few years ago, but mostly, doors are well bolted from the inside.[1] Old Delhi is still the home of traditional *hijra* households. In the suburban townships of Gurgaon and Noida, there is always the possibility of a queer mall culture developing. But the most likely place is the center of town.

It's my guess that this center is going to be Connaught Place. It has a historical association as a meeting place for gay men. It's in a genre well understood globally—a central park in a large city. You don't need a guidebook to find it. It's sited at the intersection of old and new Delhi and is rapidly becoming the symbolic center as the crossing point for the Delhi Metro. We seem to know our modern cities by their public-transport system maps. We also know that India will not be modern nor shining if it does not include the geographies of freedom. So now, it's up to us to come outside and reclaim our streets. You can help by joining in the Nigah Picnic, a public affirmation of a queer space.[2]

## WHAT KIND OF MAN ARE YOU?

After decades of women self-reflecting, giving rise to the women's movement and consequently to the lesbian/gay movement, men are finally beginning to take part in the conversation. Delhi is the venue for a large number of discussions, film screenings, and even an art show discussing "masculinities." So are the guys fifty years too late? And where have they been all this time?

But wait a minute, this is not necessarily about and by men; it's more about their gender identity, and it's the lessons they can learn from the rest of us. And they need to learn these lessons,

   *QUEERING THE INDIAN STREET*

we're being told, if the world is to become a safer place. But who are "they" and who is "us"? By implication, "they" are heterosexual men and "us" is everybody else, including homosexual men. Sensitive, thinking, straight men are not included; they've already been deemed queer. They even get invited to Nigah parties and sometimes want to marry queer women.

There are many reasons why boys who will be boys get that way. Let's consider one very important facet that we discussed the other day in the hallowed halls of St. Stephen's College: homophobia. While we may be biologically distinguishable at birth in our nakedness, our gender starts being forced down our throats at a very early age. It's in everything—our dress codes for babies, our haircuts, and so on. This early part seems fairly easy, as usually we don't really participate in making choices; we are just hapless victims having to endure our parents' wishes.

The trouble starts at puberty. All this unseemly hair appears and needs covering up, so out go shorts and from then on, it's trousers and long sleeves. And suddenly the playground, that nice friendly place, becomes a menacing battleground for who is going to be the alpha male on the block. Mothers give way to fathers as role models and guides on the road to masculinity and world dominance. But by then, there is a hitch in this smooth transition. Sex—no one told us about it and no one warned us that it would unleash its ugly desire and get us all into a mess on our journey into masculinity. What if we actually desired other boys?

That, we knew, without being told almost, was completely unacceptable. You could never be the alpha male if you were the school fag. You would never head a corporation or a country. Oh, you could excel at sports and in the science classes, and date the prettiest girls, but there couldn't be a whiff of questioning hovering over your desire for another man. The mere mention of the subject brings out your most deep-seated fears. And it's a terrifying, irrational fear. And when you come across anyone that might dare to display such desire, you might respond in the most violent way.

This is not a subject that you can discuss politely in a forum, or at a film screening or an art gallery. This touches your own inner being. Queer men and women know that most subtle of differences between heterosexism, which makes us underprivileged, and homophobia, which can make us fear for our lives. So if you're not prepared to discuss the most serious challenge to your masculinity, what kind of man are you?

## CONNAUGHT PLACE

Connaught Place (CP). The very name used to arouse a certain excitement. Growing up in the 1960s, hearing about it from one's parents, being taken there for everything from school uniforms to visits to the doctor, to having one's official family portrait taken in a photo studio. An outing to CP spelled glamour and excitement and a break from the somewhat predictable routines of life in the colony. Of course, I was fortunate that school lay on the other side of it, so once I was old enough to be free of the school bus, I could make my leisurely way home exploring the entire breadth of it. The school also frog-marched us to see suitably uplifting films for boys at the Rivoli cinema—ironically, mostly about male bonding. Little did we know that just below our radar was one of the most active gay cruising sites in the city.

In those days, teenage boys from nice homes weren't supposed to be having sex, and certainly not homosex. Families weren't mentioning it, schools weren't mentioning it, and it was definitely not in the media at the time. Then suddenly, Delhi's first late-night disco, The Cellar, opened on the Parliament Street corner of the Regal Building. Pummy Singh recounted to me recently how he fought a lengthy legal battle to keep it open, and how it was a precursor to the wholesale liberalization of Delhi's nightlife. It was here where someone first nudged me in the ribs (as I sat drinking my Coke, which was my bribe for not "telling on" the extracurricular activities of my older sibling and her mates), and pointed out that someone was queer. It was here that very sexy men were dancing to Wilson Pickett and Aretha Franklin and were openly gay. It was very exciting and very appropriate that it should happen in a basement in CP. Not that I could do much about it at the time—as I wasn't ready to be identified as queer—except observe and try and connect it to what was happening on the streets and park outside.

Outside, a very different world operated. It was free of class and "niceness." Men were on the prowl for sex, just that. No nice conversation, no attitude about class and connections. Just raunchy, instantly available sex. Here, one could have sex and not worry about labels, since no one was talking. It didn't mean you were gay or queer or even "MSM"—this latest label beloved of international funding agencies. You were simply engaging in what men did. It was no accident that CP functioned as a meeting ground for men of all classes united in their search for sexual gratification. It's the same in most metropolitan centers, in India and abroad.

This is true of the Gateway in Mumbai, of Piccadilly Circus in London, of Times Square in New York, and so on, the list is endless. An unwritten secret code seems to operate and cross all manner of national and class boundaries. Everyone seems to know where to go and how to connect with like-minded people. When it comes time to write a queer demographic of Delhi in the twentieth century, I imagine that the center will be CP.

Somewhere along the way though, CP fell out of use, the middle and upper-middle classes abandoned it. And it fell into a decay. Queer spaces sprang up elsewhere, and like many other services in this city, offered a more localized neighborhood brand of facility. CP acquired a rougher and tougher edge. Now, only the very desperate and the very brave venture into its parks and alleyways. A brief encounter can turn into a gang rape—a crime without a victim, as silenced and ignored. Being roughed up by straight boys looking for entertainment or a quick buck is never reported as a homophobic hate crime.

But returning there very recently, one can see the winds of change. The whole area is being given a facelift. As the hub of the Delhi Metro network, it's now become the most accessible of all the queer sites in Delhi. One can see how people of all classes will once more mingle and seek out pleasure. And a huge part of the pleasure will be in discovering each other. People are once more outgrowing what the class and the neighborhood can provide. And queer people here, like elsewhere, are at the forefront of this social revolution.

Originally published as columns in *Time Out Delhi*, Autumn 2009.

Notes

1   Editor's note: On August 14, 2004, two gay men, Pushkin Chandra and his partner Kuldeep, were murdered in their home in Anand Lok, South Delhi, by two other men. In 2010, the two men were sentenced to life in prison for the murder.

2   Editor's note: Nigah is a queer activist group in Delhi, founded by students based at Jawaharlal Nehru University in 2003. Gupta became an active member of the group in 2006.

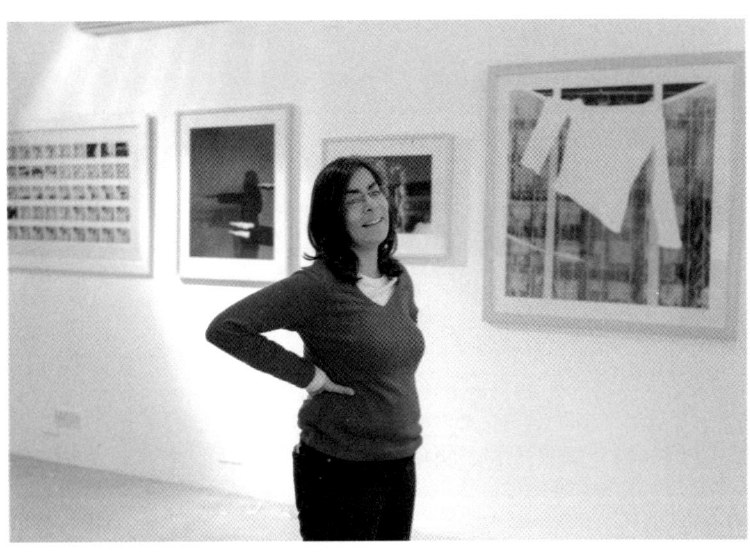

Sunil Gupta, Radhika Singh, cocurator of *Click! Contemporary Photography in India*, Vadehra Art Gallery, Delhi, 2008

# *Where Three Dreams Cross*

"What is a photograph?" one may well ask. Existing in space and by definition about the past, dual in nature in that it is only slightly codified and open to subjective interpretations, although purportedly telling a single "truth." What was there in front of the apparatus, the camera, must have been there, whether it was a person, a scene, or an object. Without that initial act of recording a trace, there would not be a photograph.

India, Pakistan, and Bangladesh are distinctive countries that for centuries shared a culture defined by three of the greatest rivers in the world—the Ganga, the Indus, and the Brahmaputra. Some of the world's oldest civilizations can be found here, and today, the populations total over one and a half billion people. So it might seem rash to trace the trajectory of photography in such a vast and complex region in one exhibition. In the absence of well-documented histories, we took an alternative route—looking at photographs made by contemporary living photographers and artists, and trying to excavate their antecedents as far as it was possible. *Where Three Dreams Cross* is organized into five threads: the portrait, the family, the street, the body politic, and the performance.

In the 1830s, both Henry Fox Talbot and Louis Daguerre invented processes that claimed to be the origin of photography, by fixing a positive image that was traced by light. Very rapidly, the apparatus required to make such an image arrived in British India. By 1840, the first advertisement appeared for this proto-camera in a Calcutta newspaper, but it wasn't until the 1850s that the earliest photographs were being made to document the extent of empire. What became known as the Archaeological Survey of India came into being. Immediately, the Native population became fascinated by this method of reproduction; while the colonizers were interested in views to send home, the Natives were interested in views of themselves. Portraiture, a very powerful strand of contemporary photography in the three countries today, stretches back and dovetails into the style of Indian miniature painting, which in itself was an influencing force on early photographic images.

In this exhibition, we have only selected photographs made by people who live/d and work/ed in the region. The primary research has stayed within the three modern states involved. Many hundreds of practitioners were contacted to submit their work by any means possible, and almost half were seen in person. Shahidul Alam and Hammad Nassar have curated the work from Bangladesh and Pakistan respectively; in India, Radhika Singh and I, as cocurators, used the opportunity to present some of the contemporary work in a large survey show called *Click!* in 2008 at Vadehra Art Gallery, New Delhi. We felt Indians in India needed to see work that was made locally. Ironically, in the period covered by the research into this project, the possibility of showing photographs in a gallery has grown exponentially. Of course Drik, in Bangladesh, has been around for some time now—running a school and a very established annual photo festival called Chobi Mela. India, on the other hand—with a huge economy and consequent enlargement of the commercial market for advertising, editorial, and fashion photography—has only just managed to get itself a gallery devoted exclusively to photography, and has yet to create even a national-level festival. Meanwhile, the Indian art market took off, and hanging on to its coattails was the market for photographic prints.

Suddenly, not only was Indian art everywhere, but Indian photography was making an appearance, ushered in, as it were, by a major presence in the Rencontres d'Arles festival of 2007. And there it was, in the international auction houses of London, New York, and Paris. No longer was it a well-kept secret. However, the vexed question remains: What is Indian photography and what might be "good" Indian photography (leaving aside the rather more mundane issue of value as determined by the auctioneers)? And as the Indian art market boomed, so did South Asia's. Names previously unfamiliar on the international scene, like Rashid Rana and Pushpamala N., were commandeering an audience and a market. And photojournalists like Munem Wasif and Pablo Bartholomew were having solo shows in the US and Europe. Back in India, there was a flood of solo and group shows and a mushrooming of monographs and catalogues, a few years ago, one might have said, "But where are the books?" Now, they fill nearly two shelves of my library.

Of course, one still says, "But where are the *history* books?" These have yet to be written. Photography as an academic discipline is still in its infancy on the subcontinent. Virtually everyone who has studied has had to go abroad. While there have been technical schools and a well-established trade practice of mentoring and learning on the job, there hasn't been that plethora of academic courses that swept across Europe, the United States, and Canada in the 1970s. The first MFA in photography is finally underway at the National Institute of Design, Ahmedabad, India, in collaboration with the University for the Creative Arts, Farnham, UK.

While the nineteenth-century history of photography about India by colonial photographers is well known, as it's been archived and documented for some time now, little is known about indigenous photographers, aside from Lala Deen Dayal in Hyderabad. However, even a cursory stroll in a regional town of any size will reveal the photographic remains of various camera clubs, high-street studios (some of which continue to exist), and house clearances. Regrettably, the archives of early and mid-twentieth-century photographers have nowhere obvious to go. Some, like Sunil Janah, have left the country and taken their archive with them. Others, like Kulwant Roy, have come to light, as they are fortunate to have heirs that are knowledgeable and able to find the financial means to support them. Indigenous collections are coming of age. The Alkazi Collection in New Delhi now houses the entire and very extensive archive of largely nineteenth-century works. The Abhishek Poddar Collection, Bangalore, includes a growing collection of early works and is unique as a repository of contemporary photography; under the auspices of Tasveer, it also tours five or six shows a year to the four major Indian metropolitan centers.

The essays included here have brought together several important threads. Christopher Pinney has connected the performative nature of one kind of "Indian" photography by looking from Pushpamala N.'s work back to Umrao Singh Sher-Gil, via the studio photographers of rural and small-town central India. Sabeena Gadihoke has elaborated on how the Indian street at once presents personal and public space, how confounding this phenomenon was to a Western gaze, and how Indigenous photographers have dealt with it—burdened as they are with the legacy of Henri Cartier-Bresson in India and the consequent impact of photo agencies like Magnum and Contact, as well as the magazine world of Time-Life, on India's many press photographers: Raghu Rai, the brothers T. S. Satyan and T. S. Nagarajan, and the independent photographer Raghubir Singh, who worked against the grain by using color. Gadihoke elaborates on the current generation of photographers who have sought a more contemplative perspective: Gauri Gill, Sheba Chhachhi, Bharat Sikka, and Dayanita Singh, weaving together the bonds of family with the development of photography in the subcontinent. Geeta Kapur has written on familial narratives—the Sher-Gils, the Bartholomews—and on Ketaki Sheth and Dayanita Singh.

Returning to the question of what Indian, Pakistani, or Bangladeshi photography might be, one is reminded of what

Stuart Hall once said, that a black camera in the hands of a black man does not necessarily produce Black photography.[1] It is also a question of theoretical positioning. As one of the cofounders of Autograph, I can recall that we made a choice twenty years ago in London to focus on the issue of race, not as subject matter but as the color of the practitioner, and left it open to them to work out their own myriad practices. I suspect that the same might be applied here, in India, and that the next generation of indigenous photographers will work out their own agendas once photography has been set free from the modernist legacy set by Europe and North America. What we have in this exhibition are selected bodies of work and the histories that have emerged from this "burden of representation," as John Tagg called it.[2] While they set the agendas for their respective countries, there is still a sense that they have to represent where they come from; inevitably, this position will in turn be challenged from within by a new generation in the twenty-first century, who will have the opportunity to create an indigenous critical position that the current generation did not.

This piece was coauthored with Radikha Singh, and originally appeared in *Where Three Dreams Cross: 150 Years of Photography from India, Pakistan and Bangladesh* (Steidl, 2010).

Notes

1    Stuart Hall, *An Interview*, dir. Sunil Gupta, Autograph ABP, 2003, 90 minutes.

2    John Tagg, *The Burden of Representation: Essays on Photographies and Histories* (London: Macmillan Education, 1988), p. 2.

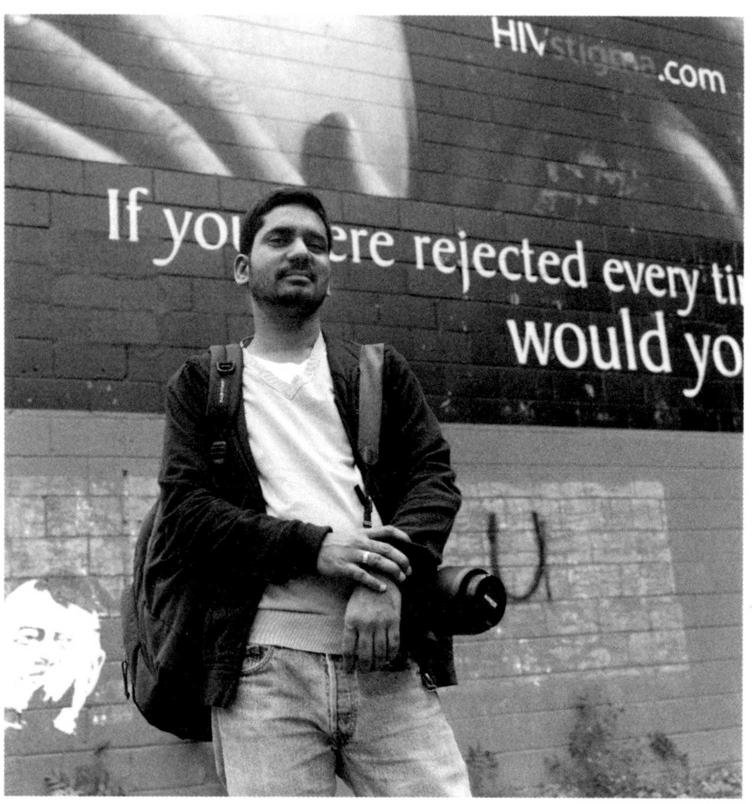


Sunil Gupta, Charan Singh, Toronto, 2011

# *Notes on Charan Singh's* Kothis, Hijras, Giriyas and Others

Although the history of photography is relatively young, the history of sexuality is as old as humanity. India tends to be like that too, a young nation-state sitting within an ancient cultural history. For second-generation, post-independence Indians like Charan Singh, this is the moment to reexamine their society, a moment to question where it is going and what layers of colonization must be uncovered to move on.

The British introduced the label of "homosexuality" to same-sex behavior in India and then promptly criminalized it in 1860. This had no precedent in the Indian subcontinent. This law remains in place to this day, although India achieved independence seventy years ago. "Homosexuals" are still criminals. However, times change. The twentieth century saw the arrival of "lesbians and gays," and in the last decade, "queer" and "trans" have also arrived. All this is mainly relevant to and driven by the English-speaking elite in India—who are the primary beneficiaries of these developments.

For a non-English speaker like Charan Singh, this overarching context was largely irrelevant. His world was defined by indigenous languages and the very specific references carried with them. These could not just be reduced to "homosexual" and "gay," terms that sat better within the English-speaking middle class—a class that has globalizing, neoliberal aspirations. He grew up with identities like "hijra," "kothi," and "giriya" around him. (*Kothis* are effeminate, underprivileged, homosexual men; *hijras* are eunuchs; and *giriyas* are partners of *kothis* and *hijras*.) These were his peers and the people he identified with. Although they had sometimes been subject to the gaze of artists and photographers, both Indian and foreign, they had never had an opportunity to author their own stories, to make their own images. This is the point at which Singh arrives with *Kothis, Hijras, Giriyas and Others* (2013–ongoing), to change the language of the discourse and to challenge who has the power to narrate whose story.

Singh was born and grew up in Delhi in the 1980s and came of age in the 1990s, just as another Singh, V. P., was sowing the seeds of neoliberalism in India after decades of being a planned economy. Unfortunately, these were also the decades when HIV/AIDS arrived. This, in turn, spawned an enormous and influential industry of HIV NGOs that took hold in India and provided a platform for public debate around sexual practices.

Public-policy formulation involves the need to generate data from people, and this health crisis was no different, with one exception: it involved a population that did not exist on paper, except as criminals. In response, the national government and international UN agencies funded NGOs that were tasked to collect data on sexual practices in the field. Years of silence and denial on the subcontinent meant that a lot of work had to be done, and quickly. The NGOs provided "drop-in" centers for men, who were loosely defined into yet another funding category, "MSM" (men who have sex with men); and Singh found himself, at the age of twenty, involved in a very early group called the Development, Advocacy and Research Trust (DART). This arose out of the coinciding moment of Singh seeking out like-minded individuals around him, his growing awareness of a deadly illness called HIV/AIDS, and the transformation of his social networking into a funded NGO with a remit to carry out further research in the field. He gave up working in art and design-related commercial jobs and essentially became a social worker. Now, all his images were purposeful for a different cause, to raise awareness amongst his own peers. The visual imagery ranged from photo documentation of peer-educator programs to hand-drawn comics that explained safe sex but also talked about love and relationships. "Professional" image-makers also dropped by to photograph and videotape the group, to further "represent" them to funders and the media—a world to which the people they photographed had no direct access. Often, these representations were very reductive, placing the group within the context of a victim narrative, which became part of the discourse.

After fourteen years of doing HIV community-based work, Singh's chance meeting with Anna Fox in Delhi led to an opportunity to attend the University for the Creative Arts, Farnham, UK, to study in the MFA photography course under her supervision. This led to Singh revisiting his original HIV group—now somewhat dispersed and at the whims of its funders—to photograph them. He decided to make this series of portraits for many reasons, primarily for the people themselves, as this subculture does not normally have studio portraits made—partly because of cost and partly because, where in their homes would they be able to display such pictures? The history of Indian photography is full of portraits, but mainly of the ruling elite or the urban middle class, who frequented high-street studios on special occasions. The underclass in India has limited opportunities to sit for portraits that reflect and represent them on their own terms.

Singh argues that his photography is a form of visual activism, as it celebrates lives that would otherwise be overlooked. This becomes especially poignant because many of the people he photographed became infected by HIV, and some have died, with their personal stories remaining unheard. The photographs, then, also serve as a memorial. Singh often said that the HIV NGO industry, once it obtained the data it needed to justify its existence, had no time to look after people as they fell ill and, in some cases, died. Furthermore, it made no financial provision for last rites when people died, which was often needed, as many had left their families due to shame and stigma, and so had no support.

Photography, Singh feels, allows the sitters' narratives to have a larger life that can act as a counter to the prevailing mainstream, globalized version of queer lives in India. The poses in the portraits come from vernacular Indian popular culture—television serials, Bollywood heroines. As he points out, his sitters—who are *kothis*, *hijras*, and *giriyas*—are markers of India's complex sexualities, and simply because they occur outside the English-speaking mainstream should not mean that they are meaningless. In fact, the opposite is true: in a postcolonial sense, they are the true flag bearers, as they cannot be translated into "LGBTQ+" and must be recognized as their own versions of humanity.

Originally published in *Photoworks: Photography, Art, Visual Culture* (Brighton, UK), Issue 24, "LGBTQ+" (2017).

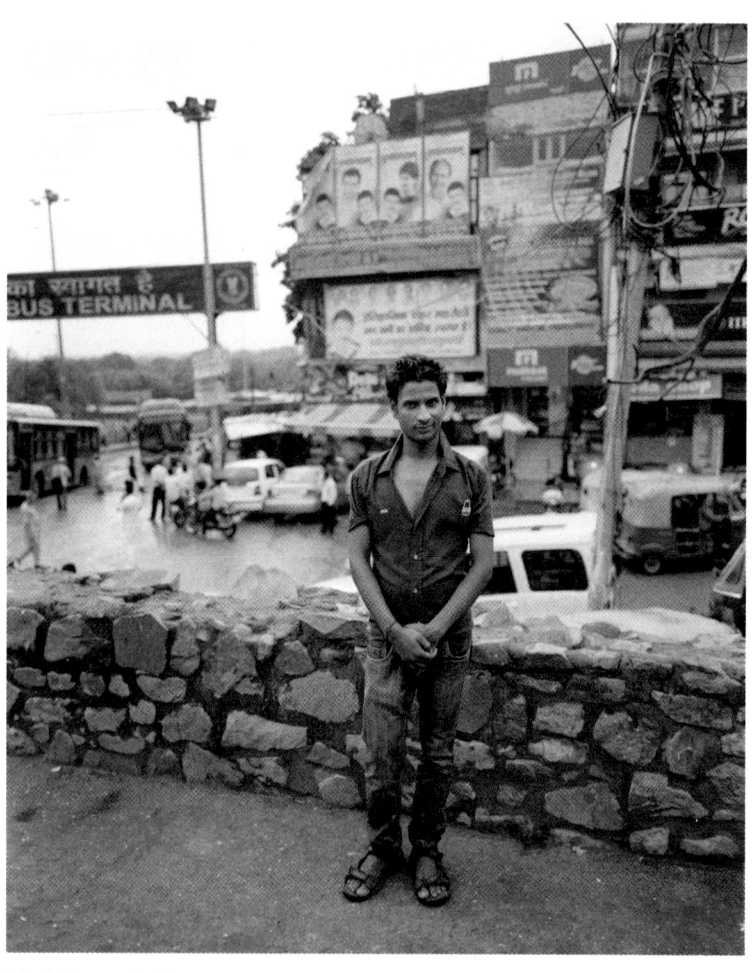

Sunil Gupta, *Mr Malhotra's Party*, 2011

*Faces of Subversion:*
*Queer Looks of India*
# A Conversation between Sunil Gupta and Charan Singh

A portrait provides great insight into the time, space, and culture of a person. It has come a long way from being a naive gesture (Leonardo da Vinci's Mona Lisa) to a provocative location of political and cultural discourse (Robert Mapplethorpe's homoerotic portraits of Black men) that has pushed social boundaries to the extreme. In this dialogue between two artists, Sunil Gupta and Charan Singh, they attempt to make a reading of their respective photographic series *Mr Malhotra's Party* (2007–12) and *Kothis, Hijras, Giriyas and Others* (2013–ongoing), relating the images to desire and queer sexualities in India.

*Mr Malhotra's Party* is a topographical survey of queer people in Delhi. We can locate this set of portraits as a confrontation in relation to society, where the sitter is mostly standing still and people around them are moving — sometimes you can see the sitter alone, and sometimes in a crowded marketplace. *Kothis, Hijras, Giriyas and Others* is a series of studio portraits, in which the sitters are reflecting on their desires and gender identities in a safe environment, as these subjects feel vulnerable in public spaces.

**Charan Singh:** Your photographic series *Christopher Street* [1976] and *Mr Malhotra's Party* have recently been exhibited together in New York. The series are almost a generation apart. Why is it that you have continued making street portraits of young queer men?

**Sunil Gupta:** I have always made portraits of gay/queer men. With *Christopher Street*, I was witness to the aftermath of a defining moment in and around the bar [Stonewall Inn] where the modern Gay Liberation Movement was born. This was a place where there was an overwhelming public display of young gay men. Here, they could safely and freely walk and mingle, dress in the way that they liked, and publicly express their desires for each other. In terms of the history of photography, it's also a time when the street photograph had been solidly validated as art by the museum world. The ethos of the time was to go out and shoot on the street, especially in New York, as influenced by the famous *New Documents* show—which originated at the Museum of Modern Art in 1967 with work by Diane Arbus, Garry Winogrand, and Lee Friedlander. So it was something I was doing intuitively, without a lot of thought. *Mr Malhotra's Party*, on the other hand, was a very slow, deliberate art exercise. I wanted to update *Exiles* [1986] and present portraits of out queers in their own city in public spaces. However, there is no equivalent in India to a public queer street like Christopher Street, so it was a case of organizing each picture one at a time. It developed in directions more in tune with contemporary times, as immediately, there were women in it and later, trans men. In both scenarios, people dressed as they wanted. It was an attempt to present the private queer as more public in India. A break from the past.

With *Kothis, Hijras, Giriyas and Others*, what were you trying to show, and why did you get them to pose like that, with lighting and studio backdrops? Are the poses meaningful?

**CS:** The ideas for these portraits I can trace back to 2009, after I had met you and had seen your work among that of other gay/queer photographers, including Claude Cahun and George Platt Lynes, whilst also being introduced to photography in general and the possibilities of what one can do with the medium. But when I looked at Indian photography, I was too overwhelmed by the portraits of princely India and the prevailing exoticism around them; these portraits were about class and caste hierarchies. When I made photographs, I wanted to make something queer but also wanted to challenge these stereotypes about photography from India. Many of my models did not have a studio portrait in their lifetime. Therefore, I attempted to create a space where people could feel comfortable, regardless of their class, caste, identity, gender, sexuality, performance; these are individual human beings, each with their own nuances. The poses and postures come from popular movies and TV serials, as that is the most widely accessible cultural discourse that we have in India, which almost everyone follows and understands. The young models have chosen to dress and style themselves with clothes and accessories and imitate poses of their favorite movie characters in their most treasured movie moments. I wanted to use portraiture as the form of my project, to give my subjects an importance which contradicted the image of their class, as well as challenged the supremacy of images of the middle- and upper-class person from India, the kind that we are normally more used to seeing in the history of photography.

I see *Mr Malhotra's Party* as an anthology of fashion, and how queer people dress; it's almost like a version of Hal Fischer's *Gay Semiotics* [1977] in an Indian context. Do you think so?

**SG:** That's interesting that you should think that. It's not the reason why I made the pictures and, on reflection, I suppose I was partly still an outsider and not familiar with local Indian codes. Certainly, in relation to *Christopher Street*, I was more familiar with the gay semiotics of that generation, also because people seemed to have followed it so slavishly. It was once said to me that it was a kind of shortcut to save time whilst selecting a potential sexual partner; I suppose you could liken it to profiles on Gaydar and Grindr nowadays, in which people use keywords to identify what they desire. On the whole, with *Mr Malhotra's Party*, I let people present themselves, and I suppose some were more "straight/traditional"-acting than others. But I couldn't discern too many indicators of sexual nuances of desire. Maybe I'm not familiar enough with Indian TV and popular cinema culture?

In your work, I am interested to know what kind of characters from TV and cinema are being referred to by pose and costume. And why that appeals to the youth you photographed and what they might be saying about desire or their lives in general.

**CS:** That's right! The people I was working with are greatly influenced by Hindi cinema and TV, that is perhaps because they are primarily Hindi-speaking people, and their main sources of visual references are cinema and TV. Art galleries and museums in India are not welcoming to people who are not from the middle and upper-middle classes, and are consequently not frequented by *kothis* and *hijras*. Many had styled themselves on popular vamps from TV serials. It shows in the way they use broad eyeliner and *sindoor* (red-colored powder, a mark of a married woman in Hinduism) in their hair parting. Others posed the way famous courtesan characters did in Bollywood classic films of the 1970s and '80s, like *Pakeezah* [1972] and *Umrao Jaan* [1981]. Because these fictional female characters are never allowed to obtain the object of their desire, they exist in a continuous state of tragic unfulfillment, and it is this unfulfillment which I reflected in the lives of the people in my series *Kothis, Hijras, Giriyas and Others*. I heard them quoting a famous line from a song, "Justzu Jiski Thi Usko To Na Paya Humne" ("I did not attain whom I desired") from the film *Umrao Jaan*. And their relation with cinema and the TV goes on and on. In the '80s and '90s, growing and coloring the nail of their little finger or thumb was the limit of subversive style among "regular" men in South Asia. This transformed into the metrosexual look of the millennium, when you saw Bollywood male stars appearing in bathtubs with beauty soap and rose petals. Meanwhile, the trend for unisex clothing or an androgynous look is gaining a foothold in India. You see the look in one of my pictures: a young boy is wearing embroidered flowery shorts, which is quite a brave fashion statement for the Indian street.

But I still feel your work (maybe unconsciously) gives a variety of queer looks—from queer feminists, students, and corporate workers to new age hipsters—which shows your interest in a wide range of people and their looks.

**SG:** That may well be so. Initially, when I first started the series, I was working with a very particular group of people, whom I came to know though my membership in the activist cultural organization, Nigah. One of the things I did was run a photo workshop around self-portraiture over a number of weekly sessions. I used individuals from this group, whom I had come to know quite well, to pose for the new series, *Mr Malhotra's Party*. They were, of course, quite youthful, English-speaking, and had completed at least one degree. The group originally emerged from Jawaharlal Nehru University, so you could say, they did have a lefty, intellectual student "look." The portrait *Anusha, JNU* is fairly typical. But as the group went in search of a wider remit and membership outside the campus, a broader range of working people joined in. Still young though, and usually educated in English. I suppose the budget and the dress codes shifted to a more urban activist look, a more up-market and trendy city look. Therefore, not the *kurtas* and *jholas* of an earlier left-activist-NGO look (although some persisted), but unisex T-shirts and skinny jeans were making inroads. As dress became more unisex, it was harder to distinguish what codes of desire were there. Perhaps masculine/feminine desire has more purposefully shifted onto the internet, and what the urban educated young want to show today is the fluidity between their genders and sexualities.

My last question for you, then, is whether your subjects, by appropriating gender-specific codes from popular culture, are using their dress to exhibit very specific women's traits (mostly tragic, fallen women) as trans men, and are therefore perhaps less fluid or more fixed in their gender and sexual identities.

**CS:** I think there is more complexity to their gender identities than appears at first glance. It is true that they embrace the "fallen women" etiquettes to lure their lovers and potential sexual partners, which may limit their gender choices. But in actuality, gender performance, including the attire they wear, does not necessarily always comply with their sexual role. Sometimes, in sex-work scenarios, these trans men have to perform a dominant, penetrative role in relation to their clients. By seeking this sexual role from a trans man, their clients are not putting their own masculinity at risk; in other words, the client's macho-masculine myth remains preserved. I am still trying to understand how, in South Asia, the notion of masculinity is suggested by clothes and mannerisms. I am not sure what it means when they say, "Act like a man." Perhaps they mean, "dress like a man." It seems to me that for both upper and lower classes of people, clothes and gendered codes of desire are now severed.

Originally published in *Styling South Asian Youth Cultures: Fashion, Media & Society*, eds. Lipi Begum, Rohit K. Dasgupta, and Reina Lewis (London and New York: I.B. Tauris, 2018).

# *Migrations and Archives*
# *2013–2019*

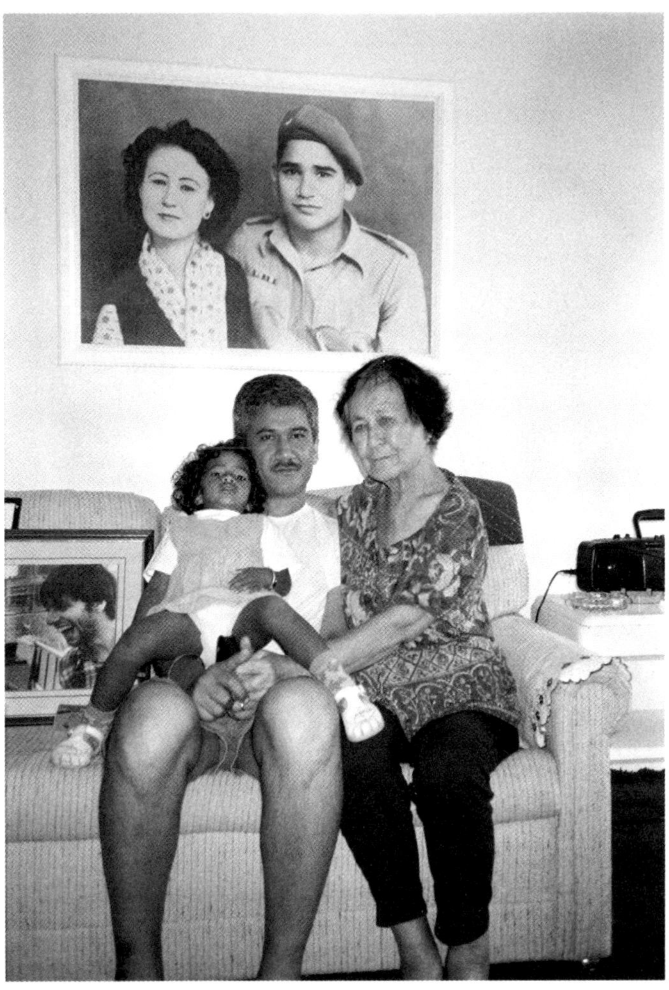

Sunil Gupta, Me with Penny and her granddaughter, Ambika, Montreal, 1995

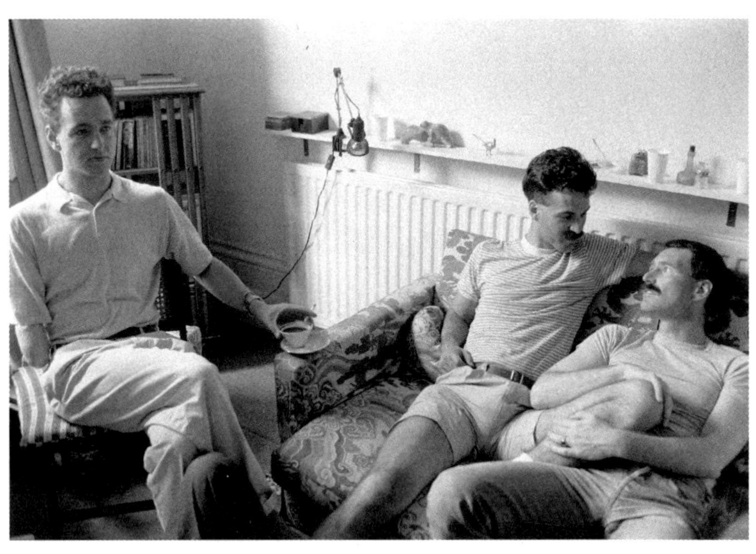

Sunil Gupta, Roger and friends at gay tea party, Earl's Court, London, 1985

# *Queer Migrations*

My first migration (to Canada) was an almost accidental one, or so it seemed to me. I never did discover if there was more than curiosity to see the world that drove my parents' emigration from India to Canada in the late 1960s. My first year was traumatic, as a senior high-school student in an inner-city ethnically divided school where there were no other Indians. In fact, India was not a place that anyone had ever heard of, it seemed. I struggled to collapse fifteen years of growing up into one. I was alienated, without even a peer group, and this did not change until I got to college and discovered my best-kept secret sex life had a name, and a community attached to it.

The two things happened simultaneously, learning about activism and learning how to make a photograph, when I got involved with student activism and gay liberation as an undergraduate in Montréal, Canada, in the early 1970s. There were a lot of words but no pictures. I had grown up in India with a camera in the family, and this tradition of the family album continued when I arrived in Canada in 1969. However, here in the West, I was able to afford a basic 35 mm camera and lens, and my photography suddenly became more serious. I began to document different aspects of burgeoning gay life, including protests on the streets, various community interest groups, pubs and bars where people gathered socially, and of course, all of my friends and lovers.

I taught myself how to make better photographs from books. I bought a basic enlarger and was able to make my own prints in my bathroom.

All this time, I had almost no other contact with the public culture around photography and art, as I was in business school. My other main activities were to go to the cinema, something that I had been doing since my childhood in India, and television—a new medium for me. I was introduced by my university's film society to the idea of independent filmmakers, and I had an informal education simply by viewing European and World Cinema. I was more interested in narrative—Akira Kurosawa, Yasujirō Ozu, François Truffaut—than in their experimental counterparts, like Alain Resnais and Jean-Luc Godard. But then the Germans caught my attention, especially Rainer Werner Fassbinder and Rosa von Praunheim, who meshed gay sexual politics into plausible narratives and melodrama, codes familiar to me from Hindi cinema.

In this obsession with visual narratives, a close friend and I developed a whole series of fictional characters based on the people around us, people that we saw regularly every night in the gay bars. The characters were given names and fictional backgrounds, poetry was also written. One day, we decided to put my photography and his poems together, using our characters as subjects to make a series of works that addressed our lives as young gay men out and about in the city. The form of this work, an 8-by-10 photograph with handwriting in two lines underneath, was derived from the work of Duane Michals.

Whilst I was teaching myself how to make technically good photographic prints, I was also teaching myself some rudimentary history of twentieth-century photography made popular by a Time-Life series of books. Of course, there was no gay or queer section back then, so one had to try and read between the lines and see between the pictures to find any relevant images.

The broader gay cultural context was better served by written art forms such as novels and poetry. We formed a gay reading group that met weekly to discuss a single work—either a novel, play, or poem—starting with E. M. Forster's 1924 *A Passage to India*. Then, underground cinema came into focus, and we began to make connections between filmmakers Jean Cocteau, Fassbinder, von Praunheim, and more mainstream films like *Sunday Bloody Sunday* (1971) and *The Killing of Sister George* (1968). In the realm of photography, we had to make do with the remnants of 1950s "physique" magazine culture and more hard-core gay pornography that was becoming available via our first gay bookshop in Montréal, L'Androgyne/Androgyny (1973–2002). Gay politics became a battle around censorship. A very important struggle ensued, polarizing women and gay men, to legally make and distribute images that depicted our sexuality. All of this happened before I went to art school.

My turning point toward photography came when I went to New York in 1976 to embark on an MBA. It was here in New York that I encountered the two things that I was most interested in: photography and gay culture. I gave up business studies and enrolled at the New School to study photography with Lisette Model, Philippe Halsman, and George Tice, and I began to spend a lot of my days either photographing public gay life in the West Village or visiting the more than fifty photography galleries that had sprung up in Manhattan. Very quickly, I found interesting gay photographers who made "gay photographs" that appealed to me, such as Robert Mapplethorpe, Duane Michals, Arthur Tress, and Peter Hujar.

The following year I came to London, and after some desultory attempts at finding an accounting job, I enrolled in a full-time photography course at the West Surrey College of Art and Design, and after five years of study, I graduated with an MA from the Royal College of Art in 1983. During this experience, both my race and my homosexuality, coupled with a certain activist stance, became a problem. There was no teaching about either topic, neither in the studio sessions nor the art history classes. I had to devise and seek out my own cultural studies program. Presenting gay work in college became a problem, much to my surprise. I was told by the administration that it was only a legal sexual preference for students over the age of twenty-one, and as I was a mature student, I could get into legal trouble. The work of the gay photographers that I had encountered in New York was never mentioned, and certainly, their pictures could never be shown. Similarly, there was no discussion of non-European photography, and there was no mention of India other than in terms of the history of the colonizers' gaze in the nineteenth century, followed by the roving eye of Western photographers like Margaret Bourke-White and Henri Cartier-Bresson in the mid-twentieth century.

HOMELANDS

*Homelands* (2001–3) is an interrogation of the geography of home crisscrossed through HIV-positive eyes (I was diagnosed in July 1995). Northern India, the Northeastern US, and Eastern Canada have all been homes to me over the years, and I wanted to explore making work about the journeys traversed between them. Starting in 2000, I began to make photographs in all these locations that I had lived in, with a view to presenting them as diptychs that might be in binary opposition to each other at first glance: East-West, urban-rural, and so on. My intention was also to present the subjective view of a person living with HIV. The HIV/AIDS story was being received differently in each place. The initial pieces that emerged were based simply on the notion that the West, where I then lived, was to be seen as the current context of my life, whereas India would be seen as slightly removed. India remained a place to which I have strong ties, including ancestral property, but that has a mythical status, as I hardly ever got to experience it for real in my adult life. Its memory was served by photography and oral history. What the audience experiences, then, are these large-scale photographs, "geographies" of home, and a videotape representing a journey between the spaces, a personal travelogue within which a discussion takes place about being gay, Indian, and HIV-positive. So, while the narrative remained close to the body, the photography became liberated to explore the outside world.

HIV/AIDS had played out culturally very differently in each of these locations. India had been a mystery, as there was hardly any news at all. In the late 1980s, the initial reaction was very negative, and I made a work, *No Solutions* (1989), about that for my exhibition and book project *Ecstatic Antibodies* (1990). Then the issue slowly disappeared from view in the public domain. It became more identified as being a lower-class problem of little consequence to the state, the national narrative being that the virus arrived in the coastal city of Chennai and was spread by sex workers and lonely truck drivers along the highways of India. Since there were officially no gays in India, the North American/ British rhetoric of the "gay plague" simply never arose; it hadn't transcended into Africa and India, perhaps because the sexuality of women and gay men was still hidden. The overarching theme of AIDS in India was one of class. I had not anticipated how derogatory that was. Instead of the "gay plague" and its accompanying rabid homophobia, the government and NGOs opened up safe spaces where "men who have sex with men" (MSM) could meet and discuss, and by accident, this created a situation where male (homo)sexuality came onto the national agenda, and it eventually led to its decriminalization.

The geographies in *Homelands*, then, vary tremendously by class. I began to move away from thinking about the clichéd juxtaposition of East and West to something more complicated that might give an inkling of *what* was more permissible, and, equally importantly, *where*. Although there is not a series linearity to the final set of images, there is a first image of sorts, the first juxtaposition that I arrived at that set the tone for the entire series. It is a view of a field in my ancestral homeland occupied by a cow and, in the enlargement, you can make out that her body is shielding a calf. On the right-hand side, there is a self-portrait in an American interior space. In my mind, amongst the many things going on in this juxtaposition is the one of public versus private. This theme has been at the center of ongoing debate in India around the decriminalizing of homosexuality. The legal right to engage in consenting sexual acts in private, versus the inability of many Indians to claim a private space.

*Homelands* began as a three-year research project on the impact of HIV/AIDS on India but ended up being equally about an autobiographical journey home. In the video, I retraced my original visits "home" as an emigrant to the land of the ancestors. I imagined, as a gay HIV-positive man, that there was little chance of a "return." Yet there was a hopefulness as I arrived back in Delhi that, in fact, the place was in transition, that I could remain here and have some kind of engagement with its future outlook and development. With hindsight, a showing of *Homelands* in Delhi in 2004 at the India Habitat Centre did provoke a return. By 2005, I had given up on London and made Delhi my new home.


## MR MALHOTRA'S PARTY


In the 1980s, I worked on constructed documentary images of anonymous gay men in historic architectural spaces in Delhi (*Exiles* series). Back then, it was a challenge for me to make a photographic series about this subject. It seemed so fraught that I never returned to it until I came to live, once again, in Delhi. I realized there had been a sea change in public opinion, and it was time to revisit the idea that gay men exist in Delhi.

In early 2000s India, homosexual men were lurking less in parks and more on the internet. Those who could afford the entrance charges also inhabited spaces such as "private" parties. Gay nights at local clubs in Delhi were always sign-posted as private parties in a fictitious person's name. Attending one such night, I noticed that the party was hosted by a "Mr Malhotra." It seemed so out of place, because it was such a common name, one that conjured up the hardworking Punjabi families that had arrived after Partition and had made Delhi what it is now. Its mundanity could not be further away from the offer of the underground glamour of a hedonistic gay party. It immediately struck me as a good title for this project, as we were all guests of an imaginary party, which I called *Mr Malhotra's Party* (2007–12).

With these images, I was trying to visualize this latest queer space through a series of photographic portraits of real people who identify their sexuality as "queer." This time, as opposed to in *Exiles*, people look straight into the camera, and we see around them local aspects of their geography. This time, they are willing to identify themselves. There was a rising sense of decriminalization in the air by 2005 that was confirmed by 2009. Already by 2008, public Pride marches had started taking place, so it seemed like a perfect time to look at LGBT people in the eye.

Although my fledgling work in the 1970s in Montréal included women as part of my friend and family networks, by the 1980s, I found myself in a more separatist political framework in London. Arriving in India in the 2000s, I found that gay politics was very much a coming together of feminist groups and gay men's groups that were forming at metropolitan HIV community centers. Everybody was focused on the decriminalization of homosexuality in India, a reading down of Section 377 of the Indian Penal Code, which criminalized "unnatural" sex between consenting adults. I joined an activist group that used culture to generate discussion around issues of queer rights, a group that had emerged among graduate students at the local university and was beginning to make inroads into the city. The group was mixed gender and became a primary source of models when I was conceiving the project, so inevitably, it became about both women and men. In Delhi, there was no single road or avenue identified as being frequented primarily by gay men and lesbians. So, I decided to show that queer people are everywhere in the city; rather than going to a gay place, I would locate my subjects in the neighborhoods where they lived or worked. This, then, began to give me a queer mapping of Delhi.

In the pre-liberalization days, when I had photographed *Exiles*, some urban middle- and upper-middle-class men were saying they were gay; fewer women were saying they were lesbian. Ruth Vanita has noted in her memoirs that "the women's movement also fostered an exaggerated fear of being labeled man-hating and Westernized if we were associated with lesbianism." Men using the term "gay" felt a little meaningless at the time, as it was not tied to any domestic sexual or political revolution; it just felt like an adopted label by some, an expression of interest in homosexual relations. The 2000s brought more knowledgeable student bodies, who had been schooled in a culture of sexuality and gender, coming out of feminist and HIV activist groups in the 1990s, along with a growing awareness of the academic discipline of queer theory often related to debates around Western visual culture. As the first queer-activist generation spilled out of the universities and took to the streets of the cities, "queer" replaced "LGBT" as the preferred term. The media, hostile to "LGBT" until the mid 2000s, became rapidly more liberal and began using the global term "queer"; even in non-English-language media, the word "queer" was transliterated, as there was no Native equivalent. Whereas "gay" and "lesbian" had denoted something immoral, limited to sexual activity and therefore not Indian and to be hidden, the term "queer" quickly found acceptance, as its larger meaning was understood as questioning one's sexuality rather than one's actual sexual preference for the same sex.

On July 2, 2009, I found myself with my activist friends at the Delhi High Court, awaiting the judgment on the reading down of Section 377. It was read down, much to our disbelief; so many people, including me, had thought that this kind of change was not possible in our lifetimes—there was euphoria. But this euphoria was short-lived, as four years later, this reading down was challenged in the Supreme Court and reversed. In September 2018, the Supreme Court finally ruled in favor of decriminalizing consensual sexual behavior between adults. In between, however, it had the unfortunate effect that many people came out and were then criminalized again. The public debate had also brought to light a deeply buried homophobia that was now becoming more overtly active compared to the "don't ask, don't tell" years.

*Mr Malhotra's Party* was made initially as a celebration of the more-accepting liberal moralities of an India entering the twenty-first century, a way of making images of the inhabitants of a previously unseen subculture. It coincided with a period when increasing numbers of (young) people felt able to come out. Then, suddenly, the law reverted to its original setting of criminalizing homosexual relationships, and all the people who had come out found that they could not go back in. It then seemed essential to continue this project in defiance of the law, as a form of resistance. Whatever the outcome, and despite the right-wing hysteria of the present regime, people continue to come out into the open and demand their rights to be free. This was a demand that was finally met by the courts in 2018.

SUN CITY

In 2009, whilst I was living in Delhi, a team of curators from the Centre Pompidou in Paris came to visit. They invited me to make a work in Paris for their exhibition *Paris, Delhi, Bombay. . . : India through the Eyes of Indian and French Artists.* I immediately thought of Chris Marker's *La Jetée* (1962) and a gay bathhouse called Sun City that I had visited that was full of Indian arts and crafts kitsch. I outlined a proposal to make a series of film stills about an immigrant from India who lived in the bathhouse and sought refuge in a fantasy love affair in the outside world. The production took place in Paris in July 2010, working with a production company to cast my "movie" and hire the technicians. I was able to bring my camera assistant from Delhi. Our main location was the bathhouse.

This project was loosely based on *La Jetée*; I retained the original elliptical form, so the "hero" sees his own death in the "beginning" and we return to that scene as reality in the "end." The heterosexual possibility of romantic love, which drives the original character, has been replaced with an immigrant, homosexual one. The nuclear apocalypse of the original has been replaced with the ongoing holocaust of HIV/AIDS. Back in the 1980s and 1990s, it seemed obvious that the Cold War threat of a nuclear holocaust needed to be replaced by a different and equally life-threatening pandemic, that of HIV. Then, it seemed like we gay men in the West were at the forefront of being engulfed by an incurable virus spread by the very thing that defined our lifestyle, and which had been the subject of liberalizing struggles through the 1960s and 1970s—sex. The whole gay liberation concept had been built on eschewing the monogamous family unit safe in their houses, reinventing themselves every generation, accumulating capital. Willful promiscuity promised a way out, a new community and networks built around friends and lovers. AIDS came along and gave the religious right and the media a handy weapon with which to beat this revolution back toward the "acceptable" norms of monogamy and marriage. Bathhouses were closed in the centers of gay liberation—New York (1985) and San Francisco (1984). Only in Europe did they remain open, where the thinking seemed to be that it was better to try and cluster all the high-risk activity under one roof, where it could be isolated from the rest of the community and, of course, its actors could be educated about safer sex.

Our "hero" arrives from India into Paris-Orly Airport to be greeted by his French lover, a scene witnessed with an approving smile by the only woman in the work. She could be simply passing by or standing in for his mother or a guardian angel. In the remaining pictures, he alternates between living out a romantic relationship above ground, in the open, and another life where he discovers the gay bathhouse and slowly progresses toward increasing degrees of intimacy with a series of anonymous partners. Whether his death is related to this experimentation, we cannot know for certain. The actors in the bathhouse scenes are arranged in postures borrowed from the history of photography, including from Baron Wilhelm von Gloeden and George Platt Lynes. The romantic scenes are set in various references to the original film—a park, a department store, a museum, and an apartment. In his romantic world, the "hero" is reading Victor Hugo, trying to overcome his linguistic and cultural barriers. However, in the bathhouse he finds a kind of democracy, as communication does not involve speech, and everyone wears the same blue towel. In both worlds, he is new, and uncertain. In India, where he came from, neither situation is possible, so both are new to him—there are no safe spaces for casual sex and no possibility of an overground and "out" romantic lifestyle with a same-sex partner.

I used *La Jetée* because it has remained, in my own memory, a unique exploration of the relationship between still and moving image. The film also appealed to me because, as Carol Mavor has argued, it is a fairy tale; it begins as a story of impossible courtly love. Love as subject matter interested me around this time, as living in India meant that so much energy was being expended in discussions around the law and the possibility of two consenting adults having sex in private. It felt as if everything else was insignificant. In both France and India (and elsewhere in the world), gay men are trying to come to terms with the opposing political choices of promiscuity and the institution of marriage. To live in the moment, to have neither a past nor a future, to look toward romantic love as an ideal, knowing full well that it is not utopia … these are some of the contradictions of modern gay life.

## THE NEW PRE-RAPHAELITES

In 2006, I set up a photo studio as an art installation during an art opening in Delhi. There, I made a photograph of a man lounging in a green sari. Soon after, on a chance visit to the Tate in London, I came across a new hang of the Pre-Raphaelite paintings from the collection. I used to think of them as being camp and kitschy, but this time, I was struck first by the vividness of the colors and then by the ambivalent sexuality of their subject matter. Both form and content had survived 150 years and are still speaking to a contemporary audience. Returning to India, I felt that here was a collective body of work, a movement that might successfully be reworked for the local context, where Section 377 was successfully challenged by a landmark ruling at the Delhi High Court on July 2, 2009.

Of course, the control of sexuality was intrinsically tied to the governance of the state, something the British understood. The origins of 377 lay in the period of British colonial rule, a period that also gave birth to the Pre-Raphaelite movement in England, in response to Victorian codes of morality and the need to classify human behavior. Following the application of this law, there was no visibility for homosexual relationships on the Indian subcontinent. What the Delhi High Court ruled was that there was a division between constitutional morality and private morality, and that the human rights of the individual citizen to choose their own partner were being violated under the status quo. In cultural terms, this history meant there was virtually no public imagery referencing same-sex desire since the pre-Islamic golden age of temple-building.

I began *The New Pre-Raphaelites* (2008) with a purposefully well-known reference to Western art history, Édouard Manet's *Olympia* (1863), by making another photograph of a man lounging in a green sari. *Olympia* is a painting that has gained a certain international currency, reproduced globally to such an extent that it and its imitations have permeated popular cultures around the world, to the point that a man in a sari in that pose is instantly recognizable as a reference to art to an Indian audience. For me, another crucial requirement was that the work should be understandable in both India and the West, the places where it would be seen.

Having made the first image, I then returned to the catalogue of Pre-Raphaelite imagery to start selecting specific works to refashion in my studio, supported by an initial grant from Autograph. I was inspired by the Pre-Raphaelites' dealing with love and death, as well as with modern social problems, and the whole being rendered in this very melodramatic and detailed colorful style. It seemed an ideal form to depict how rich and ornate cultures, such as the ones in India, were trying to grapple with a new generation's embrace of queer sexuality. Of course, this same Western tradition had already incorporated elements of Aboriginal, African, and Asian art in it, so it did not seem very far-fetched. It also seemed right that it originated in the same place as the colonizers and their need to categorize everything.

In 1987, Neil Bartlett revived Simeon Solomon's early prose-poem "A Vision of Love Revealed in Sleep" (1871)—now considered a primary text for gay studies—as a solo performance at the Battersea Arts Centre, and at a derelict warehouse in Bermondsey, where I remember seeing it. The text tells of the journey of a narrator and his soul through a nocturnal landscape where they experience visions of various states and conditions of love, until they meet the figure of Sacramentum Amoris bearing the "Very Love" in a crystal vessel. Many of these literary images supplied Solomon with subjects for the rest of his life as an artist.

Solomon wrote "A Vision" prior to his arrest in a public lavatory for attempting to commit sodomy with an unemployed stableman. This was the same law the British had exported to India and implemented under Lord Macaulay in 1860. In the century and a half that this draconian law has been in place, the overwhelming silence has been punctured only by the use of camp: Oscar Wilde, Quentin Crisp, and so on. Already more than fifty years ago, Susan Sontag published her "Notes on 'Camp'" (1964), in which she states, "the essence of Camp is its love of the unnatural: of artifice and exaggeration.... The hallmark of Camp is the spirit of extravagance." This seemed to me a good starting point to make imagery about how queer people were surviving and beginning to reveal themselves in India around 2009. The idea for *The New Pre-Raphaelites* was born, to arrange the Indian body set against this background of a queer art history, albeit imported; but, as camp points out, it is all about sensibility. The former colonizer's own (queer) hidden art history collided with a camp sensibility with its own localized history to visualize this series of photographs.

Of course, Sontag famously also stated that camp was apolitical, that it could only be an aesthetic statement, a view for which she has been challenged over the years by many queer critics. Camp elements in India have enabled queer people to survive, and they also have a serious overtone. *Hijras* have been part of Indian culture for centuries, much before the British arrived; however, colonization did see a decline in their status and fortunes. Although governed by a more positive legal framework today, their form of patronage is in decline. However, since the 1990s and especially with the arrival of AIDS, a wider public discourse has begun that includes them around the larger question of non-normative queer sexualities. Camp, in the form of urban lifestyles influenced by popular culture and the cinema, has in the past successfully enabled queer people to create invisible networks of support and resistance to the dominant heteronormative codes. With this series, I was hoping to visualize this political resistance before it gets engulfed by popular culture and consumerism, as has happened in the West, and loses its political nuances, as we look forward to life after decriminalization of same-sex desire once more in India.

*

The consequences of two kinds of migration and their intersection play out across these four works. There has been the physical movement between countries and cultures, and the singular psychological movement toward a gay identity. When I arrived in the first alien place, Montréal, I was actually coming home to an identity that was not really possible in the homeland I had just left. This took me a while to realize, and was done with the help of cultural production in the name of activism.

Emerging in the London of the early 1980s, it became my mission to forge a practice to bring my twin interests of race and homosexuality into art historical discourse. From my earlier activism, I knew I had to find like-minded people, so that we could organize and do it by ourselves rather than rely on mainstream curators, researchers, and historians to tell our stories in galleries, museums, and universities. I felt that my intersecting interests of race and sexuality were not being served at the time by the art world, as it was absorbed in heterosexual difference theory, and therefore, I needed to look elsewhere and particularly at my own communities as repositories of new knowledge.

The *Homelands* project looked back and tried to identify the different strands of memory, place, and sense of security that had provided home over the years. Security was becoming paramount, as the body had become incurably ill, and the Black cultural project in London was no longer sustainable or sustaining. It led to another migration, this time back to where I had originally come from, but I was returning with a well-established gay identity. I could not live again in an internal exile and set about identifying the new queer people around me in the city.

*Mr Malhotra's Party* indexed a remarkable shift in Indian identities; not only were these new young lesbian and gay people out and proud, but they were moving swiftly on and embracing the more theoretical notion of "queer." The term was soon spreading in the city, then into the media—and the city being the capital, the media was the national media. Before long, everyone was "queer," but only a few understood the theory. Heteronormativity was out, and the gender-queer body was in—all being spread by social media. While the Indian government prevaricated about the legal situation, the mobile-phone revolution provided people power to the cause. There has now been a decade of Pride parades in a very conservative society where most people still have arranged marriages and astrologers decide wedding dates.

Invited to locate an Indian in Paris by the Centre Pompidou for a new work, I came up with *Sun City*, which told the fictional tale of an émigré arriving at Orly to enact a queer lifestyle that was impossible in India, between love and romance on the one hand, and promiscuity in a bathhouse on the other. Located within a framework provided by *La Jetée*, it allowed me to refer the story to a well-known artwork and give the protagonist a theoretical past, if not a real one. The apocalyptic disaster was AIDS, but sex needed no language and hence no interpretation. The story, while Indian, was played out in well-known Western tropes, between still and moving image, between race and desire. The reception of it in India was very dramatic; police were summoned to the opening, and the work was deemed to be against "Hindu culture." A very serious charge in our troubled times. It led to yet another emigration. This homeland was not ready to accept the reality of being queer, just the theory of it—the boundaries of sexuality continue to be policed.

Documenting real people in real places, as in *Mr Malhotra's Party*, was very well, but underlying everything in Delhi was a sense of extreme restlessness. The state and the family still ruled sexuality. What we were witnessing was just a foray into how to be queer by a small group of privileged young people who had the economic power and the social influence to defy both state and family. Everyone had to remain invisible; in fact in a contradictory fashion, coming out was played down, despite the parades. People continued living multiple lifestyles discreetly in the face of sexual repression. The Pre-Raphaelite paintings inspired me to visualize this moment when queer passions were stirring but finding little actual acceptance. The work itself has had a checkered legacy, with different forms of censorship in different parts of the world.

Finally, in a remarkable shift in India, on September 6, 2018, the state has stepped back and allowed the courts to declare that every citizen has an equal right to choose their sexuality and gender. A lifetime of activism and cultural activism by countless people seems to have borne fruit at last. Now, it just remains to be seen if the state will allow this shift to pass without further control and intervention. Will it stop censoring cultural production and intellectual thought? Will I be tempted, once more, to reverse the latest emigration and return to the point of origin?

This essay is an abridged version of Gupta's doctoral dissertation, submitted at the University of Westminster, London, 2018.

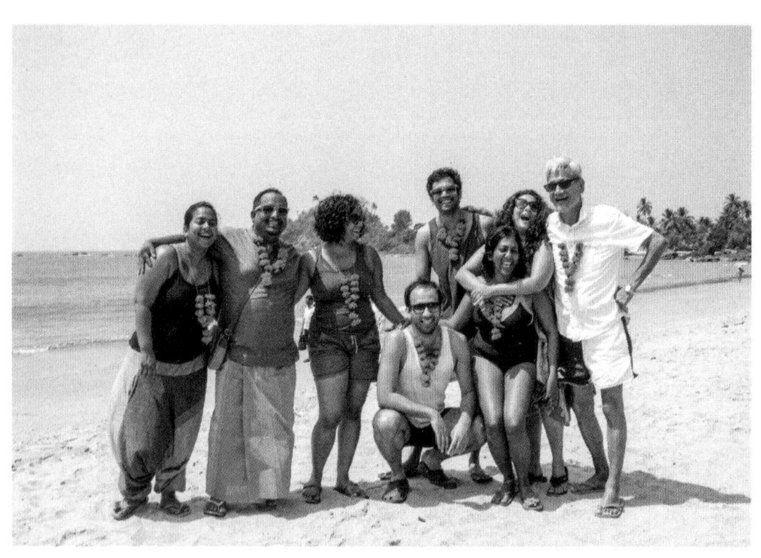

Sunil Gupta (far right) on holiday with Nigah, a queer activist group,
in South Goa, India, 2014. Photographer unidentified

# *Notes on Sexuality and Gender in Photography*

Since its invention in the 1830s in Europe, photography has been at the crossroads of art and science. Therefore, it was inevitable that it would play a central role in the social sciences, since it became instantly an apparently neutral recorder of the measurement of things and the attributes of people. Although the invention of the medium has been attributed to the competing claims of two men, one in France and one in England, one of the earliest sustained scientific applications was by a woman, a botanist called Anna Atkins, who published what might be called one of the first photobooks. Thus, women were there, very close to the beginnings of photography, both in terms of art and of science.

In the mid-to-late nineteenth century, the camera became a great tool in the visual documentation of social anthropology, both in the colonies where the "natives" were depicted and described, and at home in Europe, where various categories of people were visually categorized and pathologized; among these were criminals, women, deviant sexualities and genders. The notion that physical characteristics could somehow define an interior life and a propensity for social deviance was made popular by photography. It's also at this time that the pseudoscience that was making this possible colluded with values in art, so as to erase the individual characteristics of the artist/author in the interest of the universal gaze. The fact that this was an elite masculine gaze was never properly challenged until the arrival of academic feminism in art history in the latter half of the twentieth century. (See Stuart Marshall's excellent essay "Picturing Deviancy" in my 1990 book *Ecstatic Antibodies*.)

The American artist Judy Chicago's work *The Dinner Party* (1974–79) and the subsequent academic study that she initiated evolved into the women's art movement. Photography, meanwhile, carried on as a set of commercial practices unchallenged until the medium was brought into academia. For the West, this was around the late 1970s; and in India, this has been more recent, just within the last decade. The 1980s also saw a great struggle for the acceptance by photography of postcolonial ideas and postmodernism. Led by the museum curators of postwar US and European institutions, collectible art photography had become established as a "neutral artistic vision," divorced from questions of power and sexuality. This status quo is what a generation of the "other" set out to challenge. In the US, several women emerged: Cindy Sherman, an artist-photographer who challenged the roles allotted to women; Nan Goldin, a photographer-artist, whose narrative snapshots depicted "deviant" or queer sexualities; and Louise Lawler, who challenged the institution of the museum itself as a repository of masculine presumptions.

It's not as if there weren't earlier challenges; there were many celebrated women photographers and, as we are now discovering, there were several queer practices that sought to subvert the dominating heterosexual male gaze. The body has been the site of contestation and a mirror of the self ever since Hippolyte Bayard's *Self-Portrait as a Drowned Man* (1840). Worth noting here are the works of Claude Cahun (1920s) and Robert Mapplethorpe (1970s). They used the self-portrait as a means of exploring and staging their various identities as men and women, queer and trans. Fifty years apart, in France and in the US, but both facing a larger, quite repressive body politic. Mapplethorpe's work famously got embroiled in a censorship battle with the National Endowment for the Arts in Washington, DC. Cahun's work remained lost for most of the century, coming as it did just before the rise of the right in Western Europe.

The right to make and exhibit work about gender and sexuality using photography, something many people now take for granted, hasn't always been there. Even now, it is subject to the whimsical application of various kinds of censorship. Artists, gallerists, and publishers might be more cautious to present such works, rather than be hauled through the law courts. Many artists, gallerists, and critics have argued for the return to the universal gaze. Photographers just want to be photographers; they don't want to be women photographers, or gay photographers, or Black photographers. Strangely, not many people counter the nationality issue—so the same people are happy to be Indian or American or British photographers. On the other hand, local identity politics are on the rise, and queer identity politics are only just beginning to see a resurgence in many parts of the world.

Photographer Charan Singh writes in a 2013 unpublished essay for his MFA: "Photographs, like any other art objects, change their meaning according to the time, place, representation and context in which they are seen. We cannot ensure their meaning." However, Singh is photographing his remembered gay experiences to consolidate not only an individual memory but to add to the creation of the collective memory of a community that is still under threat in his part of the world (India).

Originally published in *Take on Art*, Volume 3, Issue 12, 2013.

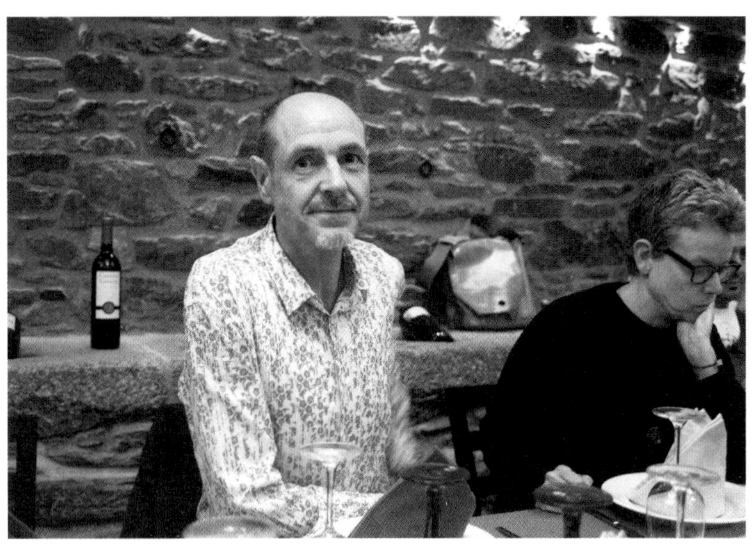

Sunil Gupta, Frank Yamrus and Catherine Lord in Santiago de Compostela, Spain, for *Everywhere. Sexual Diversity Policies in Art* at Centro Galego de Arte Contemporánea, 2009

# *Everyman: Frank Yamrus*

*The self has been understood in humanist terms, indicating
something inherent and nameable, and by extension a stable
universalised subject. It can also be understood (as post-
modernist theory has so clearly outlined) as something more
indexical, as a reflexive conditional concept, which leads
to the belief that there is no "true" self. If we follow this idea
to its logical conclusion, the self splits, merges, fractures and
becomes so performed and so constructed that nothing
authentic remains: it becomes an "every" man or a "no"
man, and ultimately the true self is nothing but a fabrication
and a void.*

—Susan Bright, 2010[1]

In *I Feel Lucky* (2006–11), Frank Yamrus has created a series
of photographs that works in a number of ways. Beginning with
an implied dread toward approaching middle age—fifty in his
case—he ends on a more optimistic note as a "lucky" survivor
with a future ahead of him. The histories of photography and
art are full of examples of the self-portrait, especially when the
artists approach a crisis in their lives. Often, these crises have to
do with the body, either an illness or approaching old age, both

heralding an impending death. This is a creative strategy very much in keeping with the Western artistic tradition of depicting mortality, either of the self or the other.

At first glance, the series might appear to be the normal apprehension someone might feel with the onset of middle age, but given the particular history that Yamrus's autobiography refers to, as a gay man living in San Francisco through the AIDS epidemic, it takes on a whole new meaning in terms of simply getting through it. Of survival and an acknowledgment of how much chance had to do with it. "Lucky," as he refers to his feelings. However, the larger question remains of whether the specificity of an experience mitigated by AIDS, already so deeply embedded in visual culture, is able to transcend that to the universal. Can Yamrus the gay artist/photographer, with his close brush with AIDS, stake claim to "everyman"? I don't see why not. It's a reductive question often put to us (I'm including myself as a maker of gay and AIDS-related photo works). As Susan Bright notes, the postmodern void of the everyman has not stopped contemporary artists from dealing with very subjective, performative renditions of their own self-image. Yamrus also stops short of traditional documentary practice by denying the ubiquitous caption of place and time, yet leaving a word or a phrase to work in tandem with the image. Both word and image then allow the viewer to make highly variable, subjective readings. Only by going back over the series several times does the autobiographical narrative begin to fall into a reading of sorts.

Photography seems like an apt choice of medium, in the memento mori sense, as it records and historicizes, moment by moment, a life lived. An archive. Artists have the ability and privilege of self-consciously creating their own archives. It seems especially political for that generation of gay artists who lived through the AIDS crisis in one of its epicenters. Then and now, photography serves as a witness, and documents the period. I have always felt drawn to the formal yet intimate concerns of Yamrus's photographic imagery, ever since I first encountered it (what

                                                   *FRANK YAMRUS*

became the 1996 *Primitive Behavior* series) at one of Houston's FotoFests about twenty years ago. I particularly liked it for the way it upended the modernist tradition and spoke of the body in the age of AIDS without creating victim pictures. The themes of the *Primitive Behavior* series starkly contrasted the anti-sex message preached at the time. In 1995, Yamrus wrote, "Issues of sex and intimacy, mortality and loss, body image and soulfulness fuel the passion of these themes that are often guised in layers of guilt and shame."

Returning to photography after a break (he says he was "killed off" by the camera), he has adopted a totally different approach, but his issues are the same. Gone is the square formalism, black and white, and that modernist aesthetic; and in its place is a different vocabulary of color and the snapshot. Perhaps it's a response to our digital age, the thousands and millions of personal pictures now strewn all over the web. As Chantal Pontbriand wrote in 2011, "The obsolescence that the digital brings can be seen as a liberation and a resistance. . . . Therefore the history of performance is linked to that of photography and its use, in the same way as photography becomes the 'theatre' of the relations between body and image and the consumerism obligatory in our societies."[2]

A closer inspection reveals a more studied approach to the candid, the camera steadied on a tripod, and the use of differential focus. So while he appears to want to move away from the formal, he still wants to make sure that he is in control of what we see in the frame. There's a natural quality about the pictures that make them seamlessly appear just as the lens saw them. This is how he sees himself, or rather wishes to reveal himself to our gaze—"natural," with all the signs of aging, without the use of a digital cover-up. So different from the perfection glimpsed in the bodies of his earlier work in the 1990s—a time dominated by the inexorable rise of the Robert Mapplethorpe work and its martyrdom at the hands of the National Endowment for the Arts, which delivered images directly from popular gay pornography to the art world. Yamrus, living in the digital age, is able to draw more directly from the internet and social networking sites, where a new, more plausible image for "real" gay men has emerged—the "bear." And that imagining is coming from the cultural frenzy of uploaded pictures with no artistic aspirations other than to perhaps find an "identity" or, at the very least, a date in the void.

In *Untitled (Boo boo)*, Yamrus is gazing into, presumably, a mirror at the initial signs of middle age—with graying hair, bespectacled, and hand over mouth, perhaps the moment of self-realization that the processes of the body have caught up with him. Although cast in a warm glow, a cold blue light lies in wait through the doorway, a light in which all these imperfections will show all the more harshly.

In *Untitled (Box)* and *Untitled (Cemetery)*, there's the pain and the irony of the survivor. The one that gets left behind. While *Cemetery* is more reminiscent of *Primitive Behavior* in its construction, the turned-away head and the stalks of grass, the coloring, and the tombstone make it feel more real. These photographs document a somber moment from Yamrus's private album. *Box* is more the unresolved desire to "play" dead. Here, the face is not averted, even though the eyes are shut, but we know that this is not real; he's lying there in his T-shirt. This is not how he will actually lie in his coffin. So why is he inviting us to join him in a pastiche of the funereal picture? Perhaps, in the face of the crisis that Yamrus lived through, there's an element of empathy, a sharing of the pain of others, but knowing that in actuality, one will be able to move on.

In his own words, Yamrus speaks very movingly about his three geographies: his source of inspiration in Provincetown, his biological family in Pennsylvania, and his nonbiological family in San Francisco. In *Untitled (Chop)*, he makes a break between the two families. Is this a return to the biological family, precipitated perhaps by the death of his father, referenced in *Untitled (Grave)*? Both these images are unusually wide in their view, taking in the autumnal cold outdoors, unlike most of the others, which follow in Yamrus's distinctive use of close cropping to just a few essential elements in the frame. Both are also uncharacteristically real. Historically, Yamrus has shown us the landscape in its critical elements—a cloud formation, a wave, or a blade of grass in a sand dune. Suddenly, here is the topography in all its natural glory, but unusually representing a moment of pain, separation, and loss. These photographs do not follow the more conventional snapshot way of "Here we were." They are not so much about the literal place.

Though full of anguish at the death of his father, news related over the telephone in *Untitled (Phone)*, Yamrus's devastation at his anticipated loss of Larry is felt more keenly. This partnership of more than thirty years dissolves in *Untitled (Disappear)*. Perhaps the death of a parent, however traumatic, is somewhat expected; even though the actual moment of separation might be exceedingly painful, there are rituals and the gathering of the clan, who now must lean more on each other. The loss of a partner, on the other hand, can be overwhelming and inexplicable. *Untitled (Disappear)* is chilling. It evokes an insoluble mystery, a doubt that will linger forever—the nocturnal blue and the closed eyes again reminding us of an impending gloom. This is a moment of recognition that a shared intimacy is no more; more a requiem for a relationship than an image of the relationship itself. Curiously, no historical photographs chart this relationship; perhaps they have been erased. Instead, we are presented with alternatives, *Untitled (Pickle)* and *Untitled (Red)*. Here, Yamrus is at various stages of intimacy with what seem to be a variety of partners. The pictures share a curious atmosphere of disconnect, of a turning away—not until *Untitled (Nap)* does he seem to relax, asleep in somebody's arms. *Untitled (Watermelon)* presents a much happier moment sharing fruit, perhaps the beginnings of a new life, maybe even a new relationship. Although his obscured face is quite telling, we have to read the moment through the action in the narrative rather than through his facial expression, which may have been too revealing. An uncertain future lies ahead.

Here, the narrative seems to be turning the corner; perhaps it's the moment of recognition that life can still be lived. Returning to *Boo boo*, he tells us that the bear image on the T-shirt is a reference to the "bear" subculture that has helped him move into middle age, with its wry take on gay social norms of beauty. This is reinforced by a couple of images that show Yamrus in various bearlike guises, *Untitled (Playground)* and *Untitled (Pump)*. By now, there is no effort to control the formal elements of the picture—these are deadpan images of middle-age American masculinity commonly seen within the subculture. As images, they are slightly at odds with the rest of the series, as they work with our foreknowledge of popular culture.

The closing chapter of the narrative seems to be Yamrus's return to the biological family fold. Perhaps triggered by the death of his father and the direction his life took in San Francisco, Yamrus moved to live on the East Coast, either at or near the familial home, in *Untitled (Window)* and *Untitled (Swing)*. In tandem, *Untitled (Station)* and *Untitled (Cross)* remember his Roman Catholic upbringing and the tradition within which his family resides. These images appear to prompt a yearning for a biological family of his own. He has said that *Untitled (Brooke)*, where he is listening for the sounds of an unborn baby with the aid of a glass, is a reference to the time he once got a girlfriend pregnant. A time now remembered with poignancy. What if he had fathered a child over the years? Gay parenting, once such an impossibility, now provides us and Yamrus another promising way of life.

Now that gay marriage has entered the human-rights arena, the idea of marriage and parenting does not seem so unreal and disconnected from the notions of nonbiological families and partners that had sustained Yamrus over most of his adult life. *Untitled (Obama)* headlines the issue of gay marriage. Clearly, it's something that Yamrus is thinking about as a possibility. But now, he is turning fifty—*Untitled (Cake)* and *Untitled (Cupcake)*—so if he is going to act on it, he will have to do it sooner rather than later. First and foremost, however, Yamrus feels "lucky" to have lived such a full life and to know that more is to come. For many others, this has not been possible. For me, another telling wide shot is *Untitled (Everyman)*, where Yamrus is gazing out on a banal, postindustrial metropolitan landscape, so familiar to many of us and one that I imagine he had chosen to leave behind but can now again inhabit. The title is telling too, no longer the "other," he is now "everyman." His story is all our stories.

Originally published in *Frank Yamrus: I Feel Lucky*, ed. Molly DeSario (Braznell, Pennsylvania: Braznell, 2012).

Notes

1    Susan Bright, *Autofocus: The Self-Portrait in Contemporary Photography* (London: Thames and Hudson, 2010), pp. 8–9.

2    Chantal Pontbriand, ed., *Mutations: Perspectives in Photography* (Steidl: Gottingen, 2011).

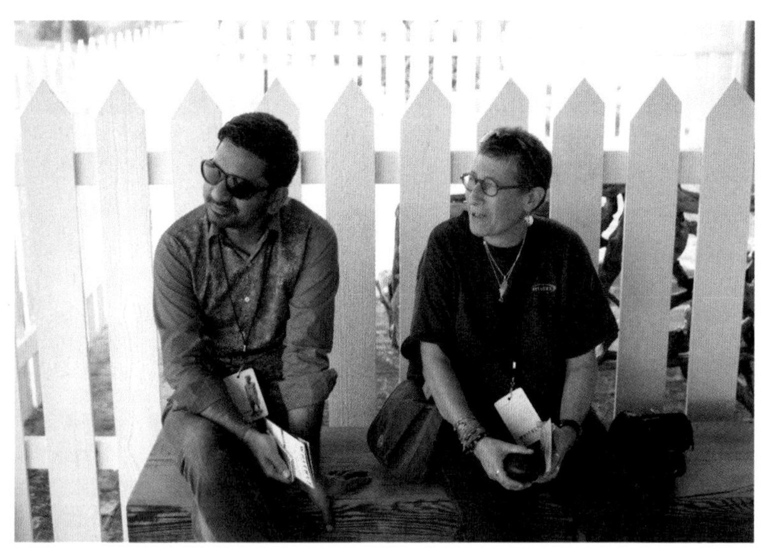

Sunil Gupta, Charan Singh and Hinda Schuman on a tour up the Mississippi River, US, 2017

# *"Dear Shirley"—*
# *A View from England*

*Dear Shirley,*
*I've gone from a married woman*
*to a sexual minority in one embrace.*
*Love,*
*Hinda[1]*

The history of lesbian and gay photography probably goes back as far as the origins of photography, but perhaps the notions of lesbian and gay as we know them in the twenty-first century are more recent. In their rush to categorize and define human behavior, the Victorians both labeled "homosexuality" and then deemed it deviant, criminal, or morally abhorrent. Photography has played its part in this visual categorization throughout the mid-nineteenth century; it said, this is what deviance looks like.

The gay artist and filmmaker Stuart Marshall wrote in 1990, "It has been forcefully argued by historians of sexuality such as Foucault, Weeks and Mort, that the sexual and social identities 'discovered' through this process were in fact constructed by it."[2] By the 1900s, it was thought that sexual "deviants" had recognizable human traits, and these became proof of their immoral and criminal behaviors.

The twentieth century saw the proliferation of photography and, with it, the private circulation of images for consumption by lesbians and gays which revealed home lives as well as fantasies and desires. However, it wasn't until the late 1960s and the sexual revolution, along with the civil rights movements, that such images were able to go public. By the beginning of the 1970s and after Stonewall, the demand for such "positive images" to counter the demonizing narratives became overwhelming. Of course, this went hand in hand with political demands for people to "come out" (and be counted). Photography and its dissemination became a preferred way to document being out. This led many people, including me, to pick up the camera to tell our stories, our way. A struggle ensued for control of representation.

I have known Hinda Schuman and been familiar with her work since 1988. We met on a panel titled, very aptly, "Partners in Crime" at the annual Society for Photographic Education (SPE) conference in Houston. It was organized by Doug Ischar and Kaucyila Brooke. It was my first experience of such an occasion, and the idea of discussing intimate details about one's sexuality early in the morning in a tower-block hotel in front of a room full of strangers seemed a little daunting. Photographers, with few exceptions, are naturally shy people, better behind the camera than in front of a microphone.

Listening to Hinda and watching the slides of *Dear Shirley* (1978–88) was an amazing experience on the panel. Panels can be dry and smart, but only rarely do they touch you emotionally. I was very taken with the work, its impressive honesty and simplicity of technique. Susan, one of the protagonists of the story, was also in Houston, so the work seemed even more present and real. It was something that I had been hoping to capture in my own work. Something not merely positive in the sense of happy, smiling lesbians, but something more human, complex, and compelling to counter the deviance narratives so prevalent at the time.

The sparse black-and-white imagery and the form of the diary also speak of an earlier, less complicated time, before digital manipulation and alt truth. The narrative is presented simply as a set of frames almost straight out of the camera, with just the text as a device to give the whole body of work a constructed look. It's worth noting that each frame is an extraordinary image—cinematic in its scope to present the mise-en-scène. What is passing for the equivalent of casual, diary-like renditions is a collection of classic photographs, each one capable of standing in its own right.

The graphic format of the diary is both a feminine and feminist ploy to counter the patriarchal strategies of the Victorian documentarians and other outsider anthropological experts. This is not an "objective" account of the victimized wife falling prey to a marauding lesbian in the woods. It's a woman's very subjective account of a failing marriage and the beginnings of a new one—albeit an unrecognizable one at the time. It's the late 1970s and early 1980s, and lesbian and gay marriage seemed unthinkable.

The 1980s were, first and foremost, the decade of identity politics and the ensuing culture wars, and photography and film as representational media played a big part in them. Ever since I was an art student in England, I had struggled to see likenesses of me in art history. It became my mission to make some and get them placed in the art historical canon, so that people who came after me should not find absolutely nothing when researching in their local museum.

The Houston SPE panel led to an exhibition in London, at Camerawork.[3] It didn't seem strange that the work should immediately cross borders. The UK was in the throes of AIDS-related gay-bashing and outright discriminatory pieces of anti-LGBT legislation—such as Clause 28, a notorious law that forbade local authorities to fund any activities (art, publishing, theater, and so on) that promoted lesbian and gay relationships as what it labeled "pretended" family relationships.

Hinda's coming-out story, whilst so locally detailed in its narrative with many references to the place (Vermont) and the weather (snow), still seems so universal in its scope. I have witnessed it exhibited in the US, in London, and in Delhi, where it was also seen at Nigah QueerFest; and everywhere, it has touched people in its clarity and depth of feeling around a very difficult subject—the unraveling of one family and creation of another.

Coming out is something nearly all LGBTI+ people must endure at some point in their lives, and for many people it can be a continuous, ongoing event, as they encounter more and more people in their personal and professional lives. In some parts of the world, coming out is not an option yet, as the threats to physical and social security remain very real. At first glance, *Dear Shirley* is about the detail of the protagonists' lives as witnessed by Hinda, but the ever-present and unseen Shirley seems to stand in for society, so when we see Hinda being rejected at the conclusion, it's a judgement whose painful wrongfulness we share.

Originally published in Hinda Schuman, *Dear Shirley* (Durham, North Carolina: Daylight Books, 2018).

Notes

1 Hinda Schuman, "Dear Shirley," *Stolen Glances: Lesbians Take Photographs*, eds. Tessa Boffin and Jean Fraser (London: Pandora, 1991), p. 87.

2 Stuart Marshall, "Picturing Deviancy," *Ecstatic Antibodies: Resisting the AIDS Mythology*, eds. Tessa Boffin and Sunil Gupta (London: Rivers Oram, 1990).

3 *Partners in Crime*, Camerawork, London, 1989. Featuring works by Kaucyila Brooke, Sunil Gupta, Doug Ischar, and Hinda Schuman.

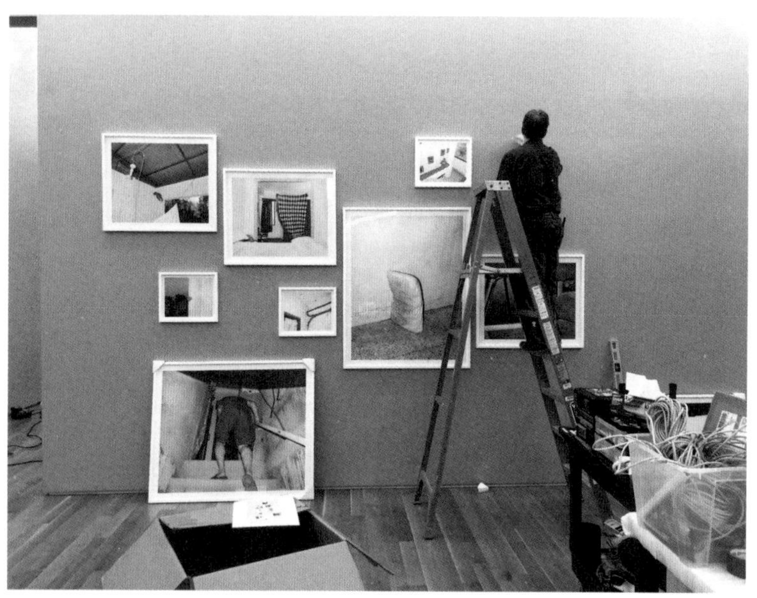

Sunil Gupta, Tenzing Dakpa's work being installed for *India: Contemporary Photographic and New Media Arts*, FotoFest Biennial, Houston, Texas, 2018

# In Search of Contemporary Indian Photography

When I was invited to research this large project relating to India and contemporary photography for FotoFest 2018 in Houston, I was very excited to have an opportunity to consider current responses by the affected subjects of the history of photography's colonial gaze. It is important to note that the focus here is on the photographers/artists making their own photos/art histories, rather than on the retelling of local histories by globalized practitioners. The key questions in my mind are: How do contemporary photographers and artists of Indian origin imagine the diverse and complicated subjectivities of Indianness, regardless of where they live? How do they talk back to a photographic history that has remained Eurocentric for over a century and a half? How do they absorb the legacy of colonial anthropological photography where the photographs depict their own ancestors? When we want to think about contemporary photography in a global way, even when considered within particular narratives about India, we naturally arrive at yet more questions: Who has access to making pictures, and about whom? How is some photography art and other kinds not? How does the marketplace shape art histories? How has the subjectivity of Indians altered, and what impact has the media and photography had on reshaping it? What impact does the abundance of images provided by the internet have?

I am also trying to unify what has generally been seen as two separate histories: photography by Indians in India, and photography by people of Indian origin in the diaspora. This has been a fraught issue. Having lived on both sides of the migration fence, I am well aware of the deep reservations and skepticism that lie between the two groups, and here I am trying to find some common ground. Just as there are many kinds of Indians in India, there are many kinds of migrants from India. The Indian diaspora predates the history of photography, and in some cases, families have experienced more than one migration. The work collected here—in *India: Contemporary Photographic and New Media Art*—encompasses this multiplicity of movement across the globe, across the Pacific and the Atlantic, from Mauritius to the United Kingdom to Canada and the United States. As Sara Ahmed has noted, "It is the uncommon estrangement of migration itself that allows migrant subjects to remake what it is *they might yet have in common*."[1] The project is therefore very diverse, as the subjectivities of the artists arise from a vast pool of familial histories and responses to colonization, Partition, migration, post-independence, and neoliberalization at end of the twentieth century.

## CONTEMPORARY

India is a very big country. It is also a young country with a very ancient culture. Steven Evans, the executive director of FotoFest, and I had to keep this in mind as we decided that the works included in the FotoFest exhibition would be selected from those made after the year 2000, in an effort to establish them as "contemporary." We were also guided, in part, by the idea that the mid-1990s was the pivotal turning point for the Indian economy, a moment that set into motion an avalanche of images as well as an unprecedented upsurge in spending power and consumerism. A country that had one state TV channel suddenly had sixty-five private channels! As India turned toward neoliberalism, it gave rise to a younger generation that came of age in the 2000s that had unprecedented access to new knowledge and an ability to participate in the global economy. The lower-middle class could aspire to be middle class, and the middle class could now afford the lifestyle of the upper-middle class, including conspicuous consumption and international travel. Photography had once been exclusively available to the upper and upper-middle classes due to its expense: as Radhika Singh explains, "Cameras were imported with 300-percent duty and available on the black market for an absurd price, and larger-format cameras for advertising were either bought by family money or from another professional income."[2] Now, in its digitized form, photography has become widely accessible to the masses. Economic liberalization meant that not only did cameras become affordable, but also the rapidly growing economy provided ever-increasing opportunities. Having missed the laptop revolution, the Indian consumer was just in time for mobile phones and their attendant apps and image sharing.

MARKETS

The Western art market had "discovered" China in the late 1990s, and was now entering India. At first, it seemed that Modernism, rather than contemporary art, would dominate the art market in India; but as the decade wore on, sales of contemporary art slowly overtook Modernism, until the market crash of 2008. Photography in India had only just begun to be shown as an artwork installed in white-cube gallery spaces. Although the performing arts and cinema seem to have been well established in India during the twentieth century, the visual arts appeared to enter more slowly into the market. Art schools concentrated on painting and sculpture, and the art world seemed to operate in an ad hoc way. The markets seemed disorganized and did not really seek or encourage buyers for printed multiples, including photography.

Photography has a long history in India, having arrived after its initial adoption in the West, with studios being established across the country servicing the needs of wealthy aristocratic patrons. In the twentieth century, eventually even members of the urban Indian middle class came to the studios to have their portraits made. Photography proliferated in the burgeoning print media in both editorial and advertising forms and was especially popular as film stills, not only from Bollywood but also regional film industries. By the time India became independent, there was a large photographic industry servicing the needs of newspaper and magazine advertisers and, of course, elaborate Indian weddings. Throughout the twentieth century, there was very little research and publication on the work of photographers of Indian origin. What did proliferate was the market for, and research related to, nineteenth-century photography of India by primarily Western photographers. Most of this scholarship took place outside of India. In the run-up to the 1990s, it was still exceptional to come across exhibitions by photographers of Indian origin, in India or in the West. One of the earliest exhibitions I encountered was *Festival of India: Photography in India, 1858–1980* at the Photographers' Gallery, London (1982). There were ten photographers, of whom Raghu Rai is the only one still actively showing today. The unusualness of this event inspired me to think about why there were no photographers of Indian origin that we knew about in the West.

One of the outcomes of the culture wars that took place in the 1980s in the United States and the United Kingdom was the recognition that Black and Asian people also made photographs. We just didn't know anything about photographers of color aside from Gordon Parks and Roy DeCarava. Almost no primary research had been done about this subject. What we did have was a lot of writing about what Western photographers had shot in India, as well as relating to what they had shot at home regarding issues concerning the experiences of migrants and people of color living in the West. It seemed normal that the companion exhibition to the aforementioned *Festival of India* show, on Indian migrants in Britain, was shot by Mark Edwards and Peter Harrap, neither of whom are of Indian origin. By the 1990s, there were both individuals and institutions beginning to explore work by Black and Asian photographers, practicing both in their countries of origin as well as in their diaspora.

What was evident in the earlier scholarship was that, in the absence of a photographic history of their own, practitioners of color were taking their cue from the plethora of images produced by Western practitioners. This relationship played out even at a personal level. Visiting Western photographers were escorted around India by native-born photographers, however, it was the visitors' images that gained agency and global recognition. Toward the end of the twentieth century, some Indian photographers who could afford to do so traveled to the West in search of mentorship and a photographic education that was not possible back home. In India, there was very little discourse around modern photography, save for the remnants of the Royal Photographic Society, and the only schooling was technical rather than academic; at best, photography was seen as a craft. Those photographers who sought a photography education had to look outside of India, usually in the West, and in the late twentieth century, mostly in the United States, as New York was being promoted as the center of the photography world. The traditional Indian system of mentoring with professional photographers still remains in place; however, photography is mainly seen as a trade or commercial activity. Those graduates who came through schools of art and design in India and had ambitions of entering the global photography world found that their education had not provided them with the background and skills required to function effectively.

Before the 1990s, India remained a largely closed economy, and its art market and art world seemed equally isolated. There was little market demand for photographic prints and, consequently, there were very few opportunities for exhibition. When I came to research my own curatorial project (*An Economy of Signs: Contemporary Indian Photography*, 1990), I found very few precedents, but I did meet Radhika Singh—a researcher and owner of a photographic agency called Fotomedia—who had ambitions to exhibit photographic prints in a gallery space. She began doing this on a regular basis at the India Habitat Centre in New Delhi. A lot of the material came from her agency's photographers, who were chiefly shooting color slides for editorial and commercial clients. Therefore, the prints that were exhibited were made in commercial labs that, by now, could make Type-R color prints directly from transparencies, the working medium of the photographers. Since few people had access to darkrooms of their own, key lab technicians became prominent and set the standards for printing. These exhibitions were supported by the Fotomedia agency, so there was little budget for documentation and equally little by way of critical review, either in the press or in art journals. One of the structural problems faced by photography in India was that there was a historical division between art history and art criticism, whereby the history of photography was focused on the pre-modern, and criticism on contemporary art focused on painting and sculpture rather than photography. Hence, there is virtually no critical writing about contemporary Indian photography in India that is widely available. However, Radhika Singh and I developed a research relationship focused on photographers from India that began with *An Economy of Signs*, and carried on through to *Where Three Dreams Cross: 150 Years of Photography from India, Pakistan and Bangladesh* at the Whitechapel Gallery, London, 2010.

In the 2000s, as fine artists began to embrace the use of media in the production of contemporary artworks, both video and photography were increasingly included in art exhibitions at galleries in metropolitan centers in India. However, there was still a resistance to photography by photographers. As in the West, the Indian art world resisted the showcasing of documentary and other variations of straight photography produced by photojournalists and other kinds of commercial photographers. In the absence of government grants and private foundations, very few people had the means to carry on with an art photography practice. Radhika Singh and I approached one of the leading modern and contemporary art galleries in Delhi, Vadehra Art Gallery, to see if it would support the research and presentation of an Indian contemporary photography exhibition. According to the gallery's website, "Vadehra Art Gallery was established in 1987 in New Delhi at a time when modern Indian art was still considered exotic and its access limited to a privileged few." The gallery agreed to our proposal and, in March 2008, the exhibition *Click!* was unveiled to a very enthusiastic response. The show was crucial for many reasons: the gallery had to see if photography was a viable commodity in the marketplace, and it produced a book, which very quickly became a key reference source for contemporary Indian photography; the exhibition also brought together a range of practitioners across the many subcultures of photography, generating conversations and discussions that led to the further development of a local photography scene. One could no longer say that there was no such thing as contemporary Indian photography.

*Click!* was followed by the aforementioned *Where Three Dreams Cross*, a very ambitious project originating in a conversation that I had with the Whitechapel Gallery. It seemed to us that our historical reading of photography in the subcontinent would not be possible without looking at all three countries that once formed British India. This exhibition, like the exhibition and book for FotoFest 2018 in Houston, was also comprised of works made by photographers of South Asian origin. Several key themes emerged and became the basis of organizing *Where Three Dreams Cross*. It seemed like what intrigued the photographers in the region had not changed much over the decades. For the curators—Radhika Singh (India), Hammad Nasar (Pakistan), Shahidul Alam (Bangladesh), and me—it was enlightening to see that contemporary work from the Indian subcontinent had its own precedent and was not merely drawing from the history of Western photography.

*

In this project, the most ambitious of all the photographic projects from India that I have been involved in curatorially, we have selected works that seek to answer some of the many questions outlined at the beginning of this essay. I leave it to the artists and the presentation of their work to enlighten us further. Collectively, in their works they are addressing some of the most pressing and urgent questions confronting Indians today, including: entrenched caste and gender politics at home; unyielding problems in relation to the environment and indigenous peoples' lands; ethnic and religious minorities being increasingly subject to violent attacks; and a burgeoning neoliberal economy that is widening the gap between rich and poor under the guise of access to global consumerism for the middle class. Indians abroad find themselves back at the center of debates around migration and divided ethnic loyalties, even as globalization makes them ever more connected to the motherland.

Certain important questions persist: Does all this photography belong to an Indian tradition that has yet to be named, discovered, and written? Or does this photography belong to a new global history of photography that is only now, very gradually being recognized? It seems strange that the second most-populous country in the world has so few photographic institutions to teach, record, archive, and engage in discourses around the photography that is being produced by its own people. Perhaps the time for separate regional histories of photography is gone for good, and, moreover, perhaps our collective problem lies in the lack of recognition by Western histories of photography that other histories indeed do exist, and cannot be treated as asides.

Originally published in *India: Contemporary Photographic and New Media Art*, eds. Steven Evans and Sunil Gupta (Houston/Amsterdam: Schildt Publishing, 2018).

Notes

1   Sara Ahmed, "Home and Away: Narratives of Migration and Estrangement," *International Journal of Cultural Studies* 2, no. 3 (December 1999): pp. 345–46. Italics in original.

2   Radhika Singh started the first photo agency and the second photo library in India in the 1980s. Quoted in an interview with the author in Delhi, 2017.

# *Index*

# *Acknowledgments*

Thank you to: Chris Boot, without whose support at Aperture this book would never have been published. Brendan Embser at Aperture, who guided it into its final form. Theo Gordon for kindly agreeing to be my editor. Anne Williams at the former West Surrey College of Art and Design, for whom I wrote my first essay about photography and who dragged me into the postmodern world. Christopher Frayling at the Royal College of Art, whose comment that my MA thesis was too personal made me want to write even more personally, and Simon Watney, Jo Spence, and Patricia Holland for then publishing the thesis in *Photography/Politics: Two*. Derek Bishton and everyone at *Ten.8* for allowing me to publish on race and queer issues when nobody else in photography would. David A. Bailey for commissioning "Desire and Black Men" for the Black Experiences issue of *Ten.8*. *Camerawork* for commissioning my essay on independent British photography. Pratibha Parmar and John Greyson for inviting me to contribute to their book, *Queer Looks*. The Perth Institute of Contemporary Arts for publishing my paper "Black Boys, Shooting Back." Gloria Chambers, who invited me to write for *Portfolio*. Mark Sealy at Autograph, who invited me to contribute to Joy Gregory's monograph. Bryan Teixeira and Parminder Sekhon, who reproduced my talk on art and AIDS at NAZ Project London Annual General Meeting in 2004. Sarindar Dhaliwal in Toronto for introducing me to *FUSE* magazine, which published my review of *Shades of Black*. Kalidas Swaminathan, who introduced me to the India Today Group in New Delhi, which led to my writing the gay column for *Mail Today* under the auspices of a very sympathetic editor, Ravi Shankar. *Time Out Delhi* for commissioning various pieces. Iwona Blazwick and Anthony Spira at the Whitechapel Gallery, who gave me the curatorial opportunity to research the history of photography in India and who agreed that we had to include Pakistan and Bangladesh for that research to make sense. Mariama Attah at Photoworks for inviting me to write about Charan Singh's work about Indian underclass queer communities. Lipi Begum, Rohit K. Dasgupta, and Reina Lewis for inviting Charan Singh and me to write about our work in conversation. Margherita Sprio for supervising my PhD thesis at the University of Westminster so superbly. Bhavna Kakkar for giving me the opportunity to write for *Take on Art*. Frank Yamrus for inviting me to write an essay for his monograph. Hinda Schuman for inviting me to contribute to the book version of her incredible project *Dear Shirley*. Steven Evans, Wendy Watriss, and Frederick C. Baldwin for inviting me to cocurate the FotoFest 2018 Biennial on India and write the lead essay.

And to all the people who have made my life and work financially and emotionally possible over the years: Rudolph Leuthold, whom I followed to London from Montreal and New York; Steve Dodd, who shared a home and his academic interests with me (even though I wasn't Japanese) for eleven years in London; my sister, Shalini Gupta, who helped share parental care and her home when I was homeless; Dilip Shankar, who triggered my move back to Delhi; and Monika Baker and Radhika Singh, who have discussed Black and Indian photography with me for nearly forty years.

Finally, to Charan Singh, who has been my very patient partner and "husbandji" for over a decade now. —Sunil Gupta

*We Were Here: Sexuality, Photography, and Cultural Difference*
Selected Writings by Sunil Gupta

Front cover: Sunil Gupta, *Towards an Indian Gay Image* (detail), Qutb Minar 2, 1983

Editors: Brendan Embser, Theo Gordon
Designer: Adam Turnbull, Pacific
Production Director: Minjee Cho
Production Consultant: Thomas Bollier
Production Managers: Andrea Chlad, Karina Eckmeier
Assistant Editor: Varun Nayar
Senior Text Editor: Susan Ciccotti
Indexer: Pilar Wyman
Copy Editor: Elena Goukassian
Proofreaders: Helen Burroughs, Claire Voon

Additional staff of the Aperture book program includes: Sarah Meister, Executive Director; Lesley A. Martin, Creative Director; Taia Kwinter, Publishing Manager; Emily Patten, Publishing Associate; Michael Famighetti, Editor, *Aperture* magazine; Kellie McLaughlin, Chief Sales and Marketing Officer; Richard Gregg, Sales Director, Books; Giada De Agostinis, Publicist

Special thanks:
This project was made possible, in part, with generous support from the MurthyNAYAK Foundation.

Aperture's programs are made possible, in part, by the New York State Council on the Arts with the support of the Office of the Governor and the New York State Legislature.

This volume is part of *Aperture Ideas: Writers and Artists on Photography*, a series devoted to the finest critical and creative minds exploring key concepts in photography.



All photographs by Sunil Gupta courtesy the artist and Hales Gallery, London and New York; Stephen Bulger Gallery, Toronto; and Vadehra Art Gallery, Delhi. Photographs on pages 53, 70, 98, and 150 by unidentified photographers from the collection of Sunil Gupta. All previously published writings in this volume have been edited and updated for this publication.

First edition, 2022
Printed in China by Toppan
10 9 8 7 6 5 4 3 2 1

Library of Congress Cataloging-in-Publication Data available upon request.

ISBN 978-1-59711-528-5

To order Aperture books, or inquire about gift or group orders, contact:
+1 212.946.7154
orders@aperture.org

For information about Aperture trade distribution worldwide, visit:
aperture.org/distribution

# aperture

548 West 28th Street, 4th Floor
New York, NY 10001
aperture.org

Aperture, a not-for-profit foundation, connects the photo community and its audiences with the most inspiring work, the sharpest ideas, and with each other—in print, in person, and online.